# Table For One

## How to cook and eat on your own

By Christopher Brooks

published by Crossfade Publishing, a division of Crossfade Music, Inc.

Table For One

Copyright 2011 Christopher Brooks

ISBN-13: 978-1461197492
ISBN-10: 146119749X

Cover Artwork:
*Table For One*
Courtesy of Stephen Schubert
www.schubertmodern.com

# Dedication

This book is dedicated to my family for whom I often cook. They are my biggest critics. It is especially dedicated to my wife, who supports all of my hair-brained schemes and flimsy plans.

# Acknowledgments

I would like to thank every person who has ever put a piece of food in front of me. I have learned from everyone. My mother taught me how to make fudge and ruin vegetables. My grandmother taught me that life is too short not to eat bacon. She ate bacon every day of her life and lived to be 90. My great uncle Curt Blair (a produce man) taught me that fried chicken and half runner green beans went really well with biscuits and gravy for breakfast.

Most of all, I would like to thank the great foodies that have passed through my life: Sally Schmidt, Kirk Francis, Mark Tarlov, Brad and Helene Warnaar, Michael and Sandra Kamen, Jamie Oliver, Tessa Graham, and the entire city of Paris.

# TABLE OF CONTENTS

photo by Harrison Brooks

# INTRODUCTION

I'm going to tell you a secret. You will not find this in any other cookbook. You will not actually find this in any book, period. I'm going to tell you the answer to the question: what makes cooking so hard? Why it is that so many people who are reasonably intelligent - who can accomplish other truly amazing tasks – cannot or will not cook?

I often hear people say: "I don't cook. I couldn't boil water." And it's not just macho guys or old married men. I hear women say this as much as men. They seem to be proud of this fact somehow.

I want you to cook. I want you to be proud to cook and tell others how much you love to cook. If you already cook, I want you to cook on your own, not just for friends or family. If you already cook on your own, I want to share with you some more ideas about what to make when you are on your own.

There are many reasons why you should cook. It's fun, relaxing, healthy and sexy. That's right, sexy. Most people are attracted to people who are self sufficient and creative. What could be more self sufficient and creative than cooking?

I know a woman who used to date a lot. She told me that she was always taken to one of three or four restaurants and she doesn't remember any of the men who paid for those expensive meals. The only date she remembers is the guy who cooked her dinner. Fortunately for me, she didn't marry him (she married me).

The secret is really simple and obvious. But, as in many things in life, obvious is not always the easiest thing to identify. "Can't see the forest for the trees", etc.

The reason that cooking is so hard and so many people don't cook is because they don't get off the couch and do it. It's laziness. I'm not saying that it is easy to get motivated to cook. You come home from a hard day at work or school or tennis or laying on the beach and the last thing you want to do is cook. So the secret is to get up, walk into the kitchen and cook. That's it, that's the hardest part. The rest is really fun, easy, rewarding and sexy.

## HOW I GOT HERE

So, you bought a cookbook from a guy who produces music for a living. How on earth does that make any sense? I guess I better explain.

In my profession, I have gotten to travel extensively. Those travels often require long stays in locations where I often end up dining alone. In the last year for instance, I have spent three weeks in Macau, a month in London, six weeks in New York and home alone for another month. So, if experience is a great teacher, I must now be a graduate student. But let me back up.

I learned to cook in college as a necessity. I was broke and living in an apartment. Eating out was simply not an option. Hunger was not very conducive to finishing my homework so I had to figure it out.

Often it was a peanut butter sandwich and a can of soup. But slowly it evolved into more adventurous delights like egg salad and homemade soup, or a grilled cheese.

Once I moved to California I was poor and lived in a sub-let apartment. I had very little money after I paid the rent. So, once again, eating out wasn't an option. I discovered that fruit and vegetables were not very expensive. I made smoothies for breakfast and stir fry vegetables for dinner. Potatoes and onions were really cheap too so I made a soup once a week. My cooking was completely out of necessity.

I got married and split the cooking duties with my wife. I continued to learn how to make more delicious and interesting food and eventually enjoyed cooking for friends and family. Again, it was much cheaper to entertain at home than to take someone to a restaurant.

As I became more successful at my profession I began to travel. I worked with a composer who lived in London so I would often spend long periods of time away from my family, living in a hotel. I would sometimes be gone as long as two months at a time.

Whenever possible, I will arrange to stay in a short-term apartment or efficiency instead of a hotel room. They tend to be about the same price and are far more affordable once the difference of restaurant meals is discounted.

Eventually my marriage fell apart. I was once again on my own, living in a two-bedroom apartment. My son would stay with me a few nights a week, but mainly I was on my own. And, being recently divorced, once again I could not afford to dine out. So I made the most of it and began to write this book.

The next chapter in my life does not seem like it has anything to do with cooking for one. I got married to a woman with four kids. With my one, that made a family of seven! So my normal routine became cooking for the troops.

But, my wife is a writer, stand-up comedian and a documentary filmmaker. She travels more than I do. So when she is gone, and her kids go to their dad's and my son goes to his mom, there I am again: on my own. Oh, and as usual, after feeding all of those mouths, I can't afford to go out to dinner. So once more, cooking for myself.

Because we both work a lot on the east coast (and the fact that we just love it) we now also have a small apartment in New York. I talk about it from time to time in this book. We are there together quite a lot. We leave the kids in California and go to New York for peace and quiet. I know, go figure! I also spend a good deal of time there on my own. So for the last time in this long-winded explanation of how this came about, once again eating out is out of the question, and by now I love to cook and eat by myself.

I have many ideas and recipes from the years of both wanting and needing to cook for myself. I clearly have had a lot of experience at it. I want to share my ideas and hopefully encourage you to experiment, entertain and enjoy cooking and eating on your own.

## WHAT I CHANGED

This is a cookbook and guide to preparing and eating on one's own. The one thing that this book is not is a diet book. Eating well is a lifestyle choice and one that I hope you will slowly find enjoyable and easy to stick to.

Diets don't work. If you are fat because of an eating disorder, that disorder needs to be treated just like any other illness. If you are fat because of lifestyle patterns then you need to change those patterns. There are no quick fixes or short-term changes that will make any difference.

So my change was not a diet. My stepdaughter decided to not eat anything that had any chemicals or un-natural preservatives. That sounded good to me so I joined in. The more I thought about it the more I really thought that this was a good idea. I have always preached that you are what you eat. So why was I eating crap?

The first thing that I decided was that I would stick to this as much as possible. I would not go nuts. I wouldn't be drilling every waiter for the "hidden" ingredients in chicken soup, or refuse to eat the occasional bagel because it might have preservatives in it.

I thought if I remembered my nutritionist's advice, I could stick to my "good" habits 80% of the time and be much better off and would be able to maintain those habits in the long term. So, the second part of this theory is that if you try to stick to anything 100% of the time you will eventually crack.

After the first week I found that I wasn't really struggling. On the contrary, I was enjoying it, eating really well, going out to lunch and dinner sometimes and best of all: feeling great – both about how I was behaving and how my body was behaving. One thing that I must admit, I was in New York for the first several weeks of this so I was walking and riding my bike a lot. I was getting consistent, albeit fairly gentle exercise.

I mainly eat fresh fruits and vegetables and fresh, organic meat, chicken and wild caught fish. I also don't insist on organic, but I try to whenever it is available.

The best advice that I can give you is that locally grown is as important as organic. When it comes to meat and chicken, I am much more concerned with antibiotics and other chemicals. Organic and "free range" are always good signs.

Fish is another story. I look for fresh, good looking and smelling fish. If it is whole, the eyes need to look clear. Wild caught is always preferable. Find a good fishmonger, either independent or in your grocery and stick with them. Get to know them and they will steer you away from the bad stuff.

Everything else is about label reading. The simple rule is that anything in a package is probably not a great idea. If you want or need it then read the label. Bread is probably the most challenging. Even the fresh bread sold on the racks in the grocery usually has preservatives. What you want to be in bread is flour, water, sugar, salt, yeast and maybe some flavoring like rosemary, olive oil, garlic etc. NOTHING ELSE. I suppose the reason I have lost some weight is that I don't eat nearly as much bread because of this issue.

Like produce, buy things that are locally made. The reason that manufacturers use preservatives is to lengthen the life of their product, mainly from the factory to the market. If you cut out the truck then you can usually avoid the crap.

I find that eating out has it's own set of challenges. It isn't nearly as hard as I first thought. I found that I really had to be a little more lax than when I am grocery shopping. After all, you can't normally get into the kitchen and talk to the chef about what he has procured for the evening's meal. Sometimes he doesn't even know. The good news is that most good restaurants are very aware of their purveyors. They even brag about locally grown and raised meat and produce, even going as far as naming the farms on the menu.

I don't eat at fast food places, ever. They do not have anything that doesn't have some sort of crap in it. I don't eat at chain restaurants of any sort because they tend to buy their food in bulk, therefore needing preservatives. I don't eat street food (in this country – China is not a problem).

I will eat an occasional donut from a donut shop. They make them fresh and simple ones have nothing in them but sugar, flour and eggs. I am not a snob, I just don't like to eat things I can't pronounce.

Sometimes restaurants are your only choice. If you are on the road for business, and you are not staying in some sort of apartment with a kitchen, then you are forced to eat out. Sometimes this could go on for weeks or months, depending on your business.

This happens to me several times a year. After a few days I long for my kitchen. I try to eat simply most of the time. I stay away from exotic places such as Thai and Chinese. In this country, they tend to use a lot of stuff in the food that is not particularly good for you, and there is never any way to know. Sushi is also good from time to time. It's simple, fresh and good for you. Unfortunately, it is really expensive.

Do not beat yourself up. If you think about it, most of us (even if we are on the road from time to time) eat a minority of our meals at restaurants (or takeout). That means that even if we are eating crap part of that time, we are still sticking to the 80% rule.

## HOW TO USE THIS BOOK

Obviously, there are recipes throughout the book. When you would like to use this strictly as a cookbook you can find them in the index, organized by food types. There are your usual cookbook chapters based on types of food. But I have also included special chapter topics specific to preparing food on your own and even one for when you are not on your own called "Date Night". Make sure that you read recipes all the way through before you start to prepare them. This is always a good practice. You get a picture of the food in your head and a feel for what needs to happen when.

**HELPFUL GUIDES**

There are also some helpful chapters at the beginning of the book that address setting up a kitchen, shopping and seasonal food. If you are new to cooking they are great guidelines and helpful hints on what to buy and where to buy them. Shopping in a supermarket can be intimidating. I hope that my chapter on the first big shop will help you though what sounds really simple but can be really scary.

**QUICK AND EASY**

I am against any kind of fast food restaurant and don't think that you should ever actually eat on the go. It's not good and it's not good for you. However, there is no reason why one shouldn't have an arsenal of menus that can be <u>made</u> quickly. There is a huge difference between preparation time and the time that it takes to enjoy and digest the benefits of your work in the kitchen. There are several reasons why sometimes one does not want to take the time or have the time - especially when on your own - to prepare a complicated meal. There are also several recipes in this book that fall into this category and are marked with a great big Q.

**INEXPENSIVE**

Food is expensive, but cooking for yourself does not have to be. I have tried to concentrate on recipes that are extremely affordable. Sometimes ingredients like scallops can be a little pricey, but most ingredients for these recipes are not extravagant. When a recipe is extremely inexpensive it will be marked with a cent sign.

## INGREDIENTS AND TOOLS

Each of the recipes has the ingredients listed. Most ingredients are readily available in groceries everywhere. There are also suggested substitutes when I suspect a potential lack of availability or possibility of you not liking something.

The recipes also have something that you don't find in many cookbooks: a list of tools that are needed. This gives you a chance to make sure you have everything that you need. Don't worry though, you will not be buying too many tools. Almost every recipe in the book uses just a few basic tools. If there are any additional gadgets listed they are usually optional.

## RECIPES IN THE INDEX

I have encouraged you to read the book through completely. Once you have done that and wish to continue to use the book as reference, you will find all the recipes listed in the index under "Recipes", with sub catagories of their greater food catagory.

## HOW TO PICTORIALS

When Julia Child says minced garlic, she never says how you mince garlic. There are many "how to" pictorials throughout the book for this very purpose. I couldn't include every cooking technique so I have included the ones that I thought were helpful. As I think of others, I will include them on our website.

Please read the book all the way through, including the recipes. It will plant the seeds for future meals and hopefully keep you entertained along the way. Keep up with other how- to, new recipes, guest blogs and ramblings about cooking, travel, et. Al. on the web site:

www.TableForOneCookbook.com

Bon Appétit!

# Chapter 1
# Pots and Pans

When I was describing my kitchen in my New York apartment to a friend, I said that I had a full kitchen but it was sort of bolted onto one wall of the living room. His response was: "most kitchens in New York are just bolted onto the wall, almost as an afterthought." He continued that he lives in a high rise in Battery Park and that the doormen receive over 200 to-go meal deliveries every day. On top of this, I saw a magazine article recently where a woman had actually turned her (bolted on) Manhattan kitchen into her closet. This should indicate one of two things to you: either that you should be in the food delivery business in Manhattan or that you are not alone if you do not have a fully equipped, well structured kitchen.

As tasty as Kung Pau chicken from a cardboard box might seem, cooking for yourself is better tasting, better for you and less expensive. If you happen to live in a New York apartment, it will also cost you less in tips (and guilt) with your doorman.

I have included as part of the recipes in this book a list of the tools that you need to prepare each of the dishes. Occasionally, I will use something that you may not have in your drawer. I will tell you if it is necessary or just convenient. Usually it will be the latter. There are very few things that you will want to cook for yourself that you can't do with just basic kitchen tools. Once you commit to cooking for yourself, the last thing that I want you to do is get half way through a recipe and discover that you need a tool that you don't have.

I suggest that you find yourself a good source for kitchen stuff and go shopping. Most of the discount department stores have kitchen sections and every city has at least one kitchen/bath discount store. Make sure you get the 20% off coupon before you make one of these excursions. Supermarkets now have at least a perfunctory selection of kitchen tools, and some have huge sections even with electric gadgets and do dads. I would suggest the supermarket only as a last resort. They only carry a few brands and tend to be more expensive than a discount or specialty shop. But, if it's midnight and you really want a zester then, by all means, go for it. Your supermarket will probably have one.

# KITCHEN BASICS

Below is a list of basics. Please make a list before you go to your local "Kitchen Korner" because if you see all of this shiny stuff and don't know exactly what you need ahead of time, you will be calling your bank to transfer from savings before you pack your car. This stuff can get very expensive.

By the way, if you live in a big city where the use of public transportation is rightfully de rigueur, I suggest "Bed, Bath and Beyond". They DELIVER the same day. Call ahead if you need this service.

# POTS AND PANS

You need pots and pans. You probably do not need a 19 piece, stainless steel, rated for melting glass set. You need the basics. I will say this over and over. One of the benefits of cooking for yourself is that you are saving money. $1000 worth of pots and pans is not saving money. I don't care how you amortize it.

**Big Sauce Pan (pot)**
This is either a 3, 4 or 5 quart pan. You will make soup, boil pasta water and make potatoes in this pan. Get a cover that fits. It's actually a pot, but get one with a handle, which makes it a pan.

**Small Sauce Pan**
This you will need for sauces and reheating soups, etc. 1 to 2 quarts will do. Also get a lid.

## Sauté Pan

This is for sauces, meat, bacon, and just about every other thing that you are going to cook on top of the stove. Get one that can also go in the oven. It should be solid and about the size of a tortilla (more on that later), about 10".

## Non-Stick Pan

Do not spend a lot of money on this pan. Once the teflon starts to come off I suggest that you through it out and buy another one. Yes, if you spend more the coating will last a little longer but the savings does not work out. All coating eventually comes off rendering the pan useless. You can safely buy this at your local supermarket.

## Mixing Bowls

These you can buy as a set. Three will do. Actually one will do but they usually come as a set of 3 and they are not expensive. If they are, you are buying the wrong ones. I like the ones with the pour spouts. Make sure you like the color and the look as you will end up serving yourself at the table from them from time to time.

## THE OTHER STUFF

## Knives

You have to buy good knives. You will fall down when you see the prices. Look for them on sale. I won't tell you which brand to buy but the Germans make the best ones. You need a chef's knife around 8". Get one that feels good in your hand. Additionally, you can buy a serrated knife and a paring knife. Recently, I found a little set with one of those wood block things on sale. The truth is that you really only need one good knife.

## Cutting Boards

That's right, boards, plural. I like wooden boards for preparing vegetables, etc. Don't get one that is too big. You want to be able to carry stuff to the stove and easily dump the prepped food into a pan. You also need a separate board (plastic) for chicken and one for meat. Mark them or get them in different colors. Do not use them for anything else. Use them once and wash them with really hot, soapy water or put them in the dishwasher.

## Cookie Sheet

Buy a couple of non-stick cookie sheets. Make sure that you measure your oven before you go to the store. I have an old oven that is not very wide and once got what I thought were standard cookie sheets that would not fit. I was surprised at the selection. Just get the right size. Nothing else matters. Like the non-stick pan, you will replace these once the non-stick stuff wears off.

## Measuring cups

You need one Pyrex 2-cup measuring cup. Contrary to popular belief, there is no difference between liquid and dry measurements. The only reason that there are dry measuring cups is that they are cut off right at a cup (or whatever measurement) so you get an exact "level" measurement. If you plan to do a lot of baking you can also buy a set of the dry measuring cups. They usually come as a set with 1/4, 1/3, 1/2 and 1-cup vessels.

## Measuring Spoons

Buy a little, cheap set. You will lose them or break them or get them stuck in the garbage disposal.

**Pyrex Baking Pan**
This is the other container that goes in the oven in addition to your cookie sheets. You will bake chicken, apples and everything else in this pan. Get a decent size (8 x 10) but not too big. If you are not familiar with this word "Pyrex" it is a brand that has become synonymous with ovenproof glass.

**Salt and Pepper Grinders**
Both salt and pepper last longer and taste better when they are freshly ground. These have a huge price range believe it or not. Don't go nuts. Fill your salt grinder with coarse sea salt. Experiment with the pepper. Keep extra of both, as you will go through it faster than you think.

**Things with Handles**
Wooden spoons
Whisk
Peeler
Spatula
Slotted spoon
Tongs (get good ones)
Potato masher
Medium Grater
Fine Grater
Soup Ladle

**Disposable Items**
These are primarily for leftovers. I am not a big fan of non-recyclable goods but I make an exception when it comes to leftovers. My least favorite kitchen activity is having to throw out old, moldy leftovers and then clean the containers.

Sandwich bags
Gallon freezer bags
Variety of sizes of containers with lids
Sharpie (for marking bags for the freezer)

If you buy everything on the list above you can prepare everything in this book. There are other items of convenience but these are the basics. You may have noticed something about this list: There is nothing that you have to plug in. Humans have been cooking delicious meals for thousands of years, but we have only had electricity for the last 100 or so.

I once had a cooking teacher tell me that instead of using a microwave, put it on the stove or in the oven, make yourself a drink and sit down and read a book. Life is too short to be in a hurry. I only have one tool in the kitchen that plugs in that I use. I have a stick blender (emersion blender is the fancy name). I like making soup with it. But it is certainly not necessary and absolutely not a basic.

## SETTING THE TABLE

Even people that only order take out own a plate and some silverware. If you do not, then go get some. When my brother was in college, he and his roommates would go to the Goodwill and buy boxes of plates, silverware, cups, glasses, etc. This was a great idea in theory. Unfortunately, the reason they did this was so they could throw them out after one use and go buy more. That way they never had to wash dishes. Here's what you need:

4 dinner plates
4 small plates (salad)
4 soup bowls
4 sets of silverware
water glasses
white wine glasses
red wine glasses

That will do it. The reason that I say buy four of everything is that way you don't have to do dishes every day and if your parents or friends come over you can quadruple any of these recipes and impress them.

## THE TABLE

In my New York apartment I have a small, antique mahogany drop leaf table that serves as an end table. When I want to enjoy a meal by myself or with a friend (or my wife if we are on the same coast) I will bring it out, pull up the leaves, sit it in the middle of the living room and cover it with a tablecloth. Even if I am by myself I will light some candles and set a place setting. I am convinced that any meal tastes better when you sit at the table, relax and set yourself up for enjoyment. It is best for your digestion, your psyche and your back.

# Chapter 2
# SHOPPING

Shopping as a single person is challenging in many ways. Some of you have no idea where things are located in the market. This is dangerous and potentially very expensive. Here are some no-no's about shopping and some guidelines for everyone.

## THE FIRST SHOP

Make a list. If you shop for a list similar to the one below you will achieve two goals: The first is to stock your kitchen with the stuff that you will use all of the time and the second is that you will learn your market. You might notice that there is no food on this list. Do not go looking for something to eat on this outing. Think of it as a fact-finding field trip.

Fortunately, you will be buying stuff so you won't stick out and look like a beginner. Walk up and down every isle and look in all of the nooks and crannies (If you live in a city like New York, your market may be cramped and laid out in an unorthodox manner, so make sure that you look everywhere).

You will find very few rules in this book, but I make an exception about shopping:

> # Rule #1: Try to shop when you are not hungry.

**STAPLE SHOP**

Sea Salt (or kosher salt)
Black Pepper
Cinnamon
Nutmeg (whole nuts)
Cloves
Curry Powder
Cayenne Pepper
Bay Leaves
Chilli Pepper Flakes
Paper Dinner Napkins
Good Extra Virgin Olive Oil
Sweet, Unsalted Butter
Plastic Bags of various sizes
Large Freezer Bags
Sharpie (for writing on freezer bags)
Paper towels
Garlic
Dried Pastas (penne, spaghetti, etc)
Arborio (Risotto) Rice
White and Brown Rice
All Purpose Flour
Sugar

If you like other spices then by all means get them. I think that most people with a "Complete" spice rack will never use most of those little jars. Spices do go bad, so if there is something that you only need every once in a while, then wait until you need it. There is an exception. Do not wait until Thanksgiving to buy allspice and cinnamon. The grocery stores will be out. Last Thanksgiving, all of the markets within two square miles of my apartment in New York were all out of both. Don't wait!

## SHOPPING IN GENERAL

Always start shopping at home. Even if your cupboards are bare, you need to take inventory of what you have. Look in the refrigerator, the cupboards, the spice rack and under your bed. Make your list based on what you don't have.

I will often say that you can never hurt yourself on the perimeter of the supermarket. Modern supermarkets are all laid out essentially the same. The meats, chicken and fish are on one outside isle, milk, eggs, butter, orange juice, and other milk products are usually on the back isle; and the other outside isle is the produce.

This means that you can walk in, turn to the left (or right) and pick your protein, continue along the back and grab some milk product and continue to the other side to buy your fruit and veg. After that, proceed directly to the checkout. 90% of what you will ever need to sustain yourself is available on the perimeter.

> **Rule #2: Never go into the center isles without a list.**

The middle isles are the profit center of the grocery store. You do need things from the center isles from time to time, but this is no place to be wandering around aimlessly browsing for food. The truth is that there just isn't much food between the toilet paper and the light bulbs.

There is also no food in the freezer. Sorry, but there just isn't. There hasn't been any real need to shop in the freezer section since the 1960's, even if you live in Alaska. Same with the cans. It is good to have a few cans around in case of natural disaster, but that is where it ends.

When you do venture into those dangerous center isles take your list and only pick what is on that list. Dry goods, pasta, rice, chicken broth, bread and a few other things are usually found there. Do not be tempted by anything else. I know that it is tempting to buy ice cream and frozen pizza and call that dinner, but I have faith that you can do better than that.

Rule #3: Spend as little time shopping as possible.

## WEEKLY SHOP

Potatoes (Don't be tempted by the bags, just buy a few of what you like or need)

Onions (buy a few yellow ones, unless a recipe specifically calls for red or white)

Garlic (one head)

Fruit (one or two pieces of a few fruits. Check the prices carefully)

Milk

Crackers

Cereal (if you eat it)

Sausages

Bacon

Cheese

Eggs

Bread

Soup fixings

After you have stocked your pantry with the staples, you will need to periodically purchase items that last a limited time but do not have to be consumed the same day they are purchased. Many items on this list you may or may not need once a week, but it is a good idea to do a bigger shop when you have time, like Saturday morning.

If you are single, you might find out which of the stores in your area are frequented by other single people and when is the peak time. When I lived in San Francisco, the market in the Marina was always busy and Wednesday night was widely known to be singles night. I knew of more than one couple that met over the produce.

There are several soup recipes in this book and the weekend is a great time to make them. If you start your day by going to the market to do your weekly shop then you can get what you need for your weekly soup.

## Rule #4: Buy Fresh Food

This sounds simple. It has two important by products – fresh food is good for you and it gives you a reason to cook. It is not necessary to go to the market every day. You can eat soup, sandwiches, and leftovers a few nights a week. But for those nights that you are going to cook something, you should go to the market. This will be a very quick stop. Plan in advance and get exactly what you need. I realize that this is breaking rule #1 by going to the market hungry. That is why it is important to get in and out quickly.

You don't need to spend much time planning. There are lists of ingredients and tools needed at the beginning of each recipe in this book. After cooking for yourself for a while, you will remember recipes as guidelines for your meal planning and be able to do it on a walk, or even in the market. Try to avoid the latter as you may buy too much or too little or at the very least be standing in the middle of the store staring off into space, trying to figure out your menu for the evening. Something I must admit I have done. Sometimes they don't have what you want so you may have to substitute, so be flexible.

## PRICES

There is an unfortunate practice of many groceries to package meats and produce in amounts greater than what work for a single person. Fortunately, most produce departments also sell vegetables and fruit by the piece and priced by the pound.

Most large markets have butchers and even fish sections. You can usually buy single pieces of chicken, meat and fish. If you don't see what you want, make sure you ask. Even if it's not on display, the butcher will usually cut you what you want. If you do not have willing people in your local market, you might need to seek out butchers and fishmongers to supplement your marketing experience.

At first, it will seem that this cooking for one idea is expensive. And sometimes it can be. If you don't pay attention to the cost of a piece of steak, or buy twice as many apples as you will eat in a week, it is expensive. Seafood can be very expensive. But, if you plan carefully, shop with price in mind and study the practical art of leftovers you will make the most of your dollars.

Even if you can't be bothered to look at the prices of items, you will still pay less in overall food costs than eating out and ordering take out all of the time. You will also feel better.

## FREEZING

Most items can be frozen for later use. Please note the expression "for later use". That means within the same calendar year. Food goes bad, gets freezer burn, etc. Carefully enclose, mark and arrange your freezer items so you can see them and you will be tempted to use them. If you have items stuffed under frozen pizzas and ice cream, you will never want to eat them.

Make sure that you divide your freezer items into individual servings before you freeze them. For instance, if you happen to buy a family pack of chicken because it was on sale, you should divide it into single breasts, one or two thighs, three legs, etc. before freezing.

You should freeze:

Leftovers
Extra chicken and fish (before cooking)
Pizza skins
Homemade ice cream
Roasted vegetables
Homemade stocks (in ice cube trays)
Soup

## DEFROSTING

Some items need hardly any defrosting. Pizza skins only need to be out of the freezer for a few minutes. Chicken and fish should be left to thaw for a few hours. If you know that you want to eat one of them in the evening you can remove them, place them in a small bowl and leave them in the refrigerator that morning. If you don't have that much time, remove them to a bowl and sit on the kitchen counter for an hour or two. If they are still not completely thawed let them soak in warm water for a few minutes. Both chicken and fish can be cooked even if they are not 100% thawed.

# WHAT'S FRESH WHEN

When researching this subject I was surprised at the lack of information or even mention of the subject in my library of books about cooking and food. Fresh, local and organic are synonymous with eating well. It seems only logical that knowing what is fresh when would help in keeping your food bills down and preparing yourself for what to look forward to next month.

This is a very general chart with many variations depending on your local climate, the climate of a particular year (peaches in march if global warming continues) and the local growers.

As you read the list you will be tempted to think that this is complete hogwash. After all, you regularly see asparagus in your supermarket all year long. This is true and asparagus is probably in season somewhere in the world always.

Because of modern shipping, most fruits and vegetables are available to most of us all year long. Fortunately, most markets will mark from where a particular fruit or vegetable has come. This is very kind of them, as the farther they have come the less taste they will generally have and the greater cost to ship, store and distribute will be passed on to you.

Most produce tastes best just after it is picked. Some are more sensitive to this than others. Bananas are perfectly fine when picked green and allowed to ripen off the vine. Tomatoes, on the other hand, have virtually no taste at all when not ripened completely on the vine and picked and eaten at the perfect moment of ripeness. In order to have great food at reasonable prices it is best to learn and get in the habit of eating locally grown, fresh produce.

This chart is handy as are the little signs in the markets. There is one really big clue that is hard to miss: price! Ten dollars for a small container of blueberries is a pretty good clue that they are not in season anywhere near you. Although the newly initiated will have some trouble identifying what is and isn't expensive, it does not take long to become accustomed to what things should cost. If something seems expensive, it usually is.

Note that some produce will appear in more than one season. When in doubt, find your local farmers market or take a drive out to the country and see what's growing and what's being picked. Pull over and talk to farmers. They are usually interested in discussing their crops and what is and isn't in season. You never know, you might walk away with a bushel of corn.

## SPRING

Artichokes
Arugula (aka rocket)
Asparagus (late February in milder climates)

Beets
Broccoli

Carrots
Cauliflower
Celery

Cherries
Fennel

Grapefruit
Green Beans
Green Onion

Lemons
Lettuce
Limes

Mango
Mushrooms

Nettles
Nectarines

Onions

Plums
Potatoes

Raspberries

Spinach
Strawberries

## SUMMER

Apricots
Arugula

Beets
Bell Peppers
Blackberries
Blueberries

Cantaloupe
Cherries
Corn

Cucumbers

Figs

Grapes
Green Beans

Lima Beans

Nectarines

Peaches (late summer)
Plums

Raspberries

Strawberries

Tomatoes

## FALL

Apples

Broccoli
Brussels Sprouts

Cauliflower
Corn
Cranberries

Grapes

Mushrooms

Peaches
Pear
Persimmons
Pomegranate

Pumpkin

Strawberries
Sweet Potatoes
Swiss Chard

Tomatoes

## WINTER

Apples
Asparagus

Brussels Sprouts

Chestnuts

Dates

Grapefruit

Leeks

Oranges

Pear
Persimmons
Pumpkin

Sweet Potato

## ALWAYS

Broccoli

Leek

Onions

Lemons

Carrots

Lettuce

Peppers

Celery

Potatoes

Mushrooms

Garlic

# Chapter 3
# WINE

Whiskey is booze, tequila is a drug, American beer is water with the taste of barley and hops, but wine is food. I would never recommend drinking any alcohol by yourself as a habit but, unless you have an allergy, or predisposition to becoming an alcoholic, I would highly recommend that you embrace the grape.

There is nothing that lifts a meal further and transforms a boring necessity into one of life's little pleasures like a glass or two of wine.

First of all, it requires that you set the table, open the wine, find a clean wine glass and make a meal. I find it very difficult to invest the time and money in a nice wine and make a beautiful meal and then stand in the kitchen, or worse yet, balance a plate in front of the television. One of the greatest goals to making a Table for One work is making a "meal of it".

So please make the effort. Find your version of a nice meal. My image is simple. A place is set at a table with either a tablecloth or a placemat. There are laid silverware appropriate for that dinner, napkin, wine glass, plate, water glass and any other bowls, salad plates, etc.

Put some flowers in a vase for the table as well. They are not expensive and last for several days. If you are a guy and think buying flowers is just too feminine, at least clear off the table of all of your junk (tools, shoes, etc). Many people read or watch television when they eat by themselves. I suggest some music instead. You will enjoy your meal if you pay it more attention than a John Grisham novel.

There are many wines and many opinions about those wines. There are magazines, books, stores, web sites, tours, universities and religions dedicated to the fermented grape. I will not even try to pair wine or express my opinions about wine (much) on these pages.

I will tell you one thing that I have learned about wine and have not found anyone in the world of wine to dispute this fact. You should drink the wine you like, period.

I think you should try everything in order to determine what you like and I think that you will enjoy finding out about wine, but keep in mind that what you are trying to find is what YOU like.

I happen to like Pinot Noir. I can drink it with just about every food. I appreciate and have enjoyed many food pairings by "experts". I always have the same thought: "A nice pinot would go good with that, too". So, find what you like and drink it. If you like it I guarantee that it will heighten your eating experience.

# MODERATION

My wife drinks two glasses of wine and a big glass of water when she has wine with dinner - rarely any more than that. That is what works for her. Just as you need to find what you like, you also need to determine how much.

Women generally tend to metabolize wine less well than men. A person's size also contributes to the tolerance of alcohol. The idea of wine with dinner is that it is another dish. I would hope that you would never sit down and have a piece of steak and 6 baked potatoes. So drink in moderation and live to drink another day.

# STICK IT IN THE FRIDGE

Both red and white wine will last for a few days after they are open; so don't hesitate about buying a full bottle of wine. Open it, keep the cork and when you are finished put the cork back in and put it in the fridge. It can last as much as a week like that.

There is an old wives tale that says that red wine should not be refrigerated. This is absolutely not so. Ask any wine authority and they will tell you that opened, refrigerated red wine will last longer than one sitting on your counter top. All you do before you serve it is remove it from the refrigerator and let it sit for a few minutes. Some red wine is better a bit chilled, especially in the summer.

## HALF BOTTLE TIP

Half bottles are about two and a bit glasses. They are the perfect amount for a normal person. They are also perfect when dining at a restaurant alone and you don't want any of the wines by the glass that the restaurant offers.

I like to occasionally have a glass of champagne for a little celebration, oh let's say for example: It's Tuesday! But I rarely want to have more than one glass. I don't think that I would ever drink champagne alone, but if it is just my wife and I, a half bottle is PERFECT. Fortunately, the really good makers of champagne release half bottles. Keep it in mind the next time a friend is over and you have a good Tuesday.

# WHERE TO BUY AND WHAT TO BUY

As I said before, drink what you like. For most of us, that means a specific varietal (i.e. chardonnay, pinot grigio, pinot noir, cabernet sauvignon, etc.) which is a wine type that is named for the specific grape. Sometimes, one likes a brand or a region or even a country. Regardless of the category, there are many to choose from. These days, the importers are working overtime to bring to this country more and more selection from as far-flung places as Chile and New Zealand. The wines in these regions are fantastic and often inexpensive. Experiment from time to time outside of your "category" and you might surprise yourself.

Regardless of what you decide is your favorite, you will want to buy the best quality at the lowest price. 10 years ago I would not have recommended buying wine at a grocery store. I would still avoid the local 7/11 wine selection. But the major supermarkets now have knowledgeable wine buyers who stock the shelves with a much wider variety than before. Because of their buying power they also offer much better buys than the local wine store.

There are a couple of caveats about buying wine at the grocery. The first is that they don't always store it properly. The shipping is usually quite good these days but cases of wine can sit in warehouses for weeks being subjected to varying temperatures (the enemy of wine). The only way to find out if your local market is good with their wine is to compare apples and apples.

Go to a reliable wine store, buy a wine that you know and buy the same wine (same year, varietal, etc) at your local grocery store and compare them. They should be identical. The other caveat is the selection, although much bigger and better than ever before, it is still not terribly deep. You will not find small producers, older wines, or one offs in the local Krogers or Winn-Dixie.

Having recommended the grocery store let me back pedal. What I am saying is that when you are shopping for groceries, it is generally ok to buy a bottle or two of wine. You will usually get good quality at a reasonable price. If you really start to like wine though, I suggest you do a little more digging.

The internet is a great resource, although there are no tasting rooms. A trip to the closest wine country is always a good idea. There you might discover winemakers that don't sell in your local stores. You will also find a lot of people that are knowledgeable and passionate about wine and especially locally grown and produced wine.

Most states these days let you ship wine for personal consumption so you can have your new favorite shipped to you. If you really like a particular small winery, join the wine club. They will ship you a bottle or two every now and then and also offer discounts on the rest of their offerings.

Most major cities have a few wine warehouse type stores that offer a much deeper selection than the local wine store, generally have knowledgeable staff and sometimes offer tastings, classes and other events. FYI: Not a bad place to meet interesting people too!

Don't be a wine snob. Drink what you like and know, but don't be afraid to experiment. Store your wine in a cool, dark place that has a consistent temperature. It's actually more important that the temperature remain consistent than what the temperature is. You don't want to cook the wine, but it will do much better at 65 or 70 degrees as apposed to fluctuating between 55 and 80. Remember that wine is food. Not everybody likes the same food and what makes for great eating is variety. The same goes with wine.

# PAIRING FOOD AND WINE

When you prepare a meal you always consider what vegetable you will cook with the main dish. The same sort of thought should be put into the wine selection. I know that I said drink what you like, but I also suggested that you experiment.

The basic rule of thumb for wine pairing is that white wines go with fish and chicken and red wines go with meat. This is a good place to start and an even better rule to break.

I love a good pinot noir with some chicken and fish dishes. Many of the lighter French reds are perfect with bistro sorts of dishes like roasted chicken. One of my favorite meals with which to enjoy a great big, hearty red is not steak or lamb but pizza.

Champagne is as good or better than hot saki with sushi. And, one of the best experiences I ever had with food and wine was an amazing old Bordeaux served with a burger.

There are clearly no rules. But, like any ingredient in any recipe, you want to have balance. You don't want too much of anything. If you want to taste a really delicate piece of fish, you would never clobber it with tons of garlic, red onions and curry. The same holds true with wine.

Once you get to know the types of wine that you like then you will also get to know their powers and characteristics – how "big" they are, how acidic, etc. As you learn, start to create a chart (in a notebook or in your mind) of your favorite wines and what best describes their taste and character. By remembering specific tastes in a wine you will be able to compare them to other wines made from the same region, the same grape or the same maker. By being specific about the many tastes of a wine and what each reminds YOU of (a hint of chocolate, grandma's couch, a smoky bar, honey, dirt, lemon, bubble gum, etc) you create a unique palette in your brain for future definition.

Try everything. If you don't like something then don't buy it again. There are no rules. After all, it's just wine.

# Chapter 4
## SALADS

Do you hate salads? Me too. That is, I did. Growing up, a salad was iceberg lettuce covered in store-bought, bottled dressing. Even the blue cheese dressing couldn't make it better. Then came the me generation and the "catch all" salad with the "dressing on the side, please". Control freaks ruined salads for my next ten years. I don't know exactly when I made the transition or who finally straightened me out. I'm sure Alice Waters was at least indirectly responsible or maybe my friend Kirk. He serves a simple salad at the end of almost every one of his meals that is so delicious that I have often considered selling everything and moving to Whidbey Island to be close to his lettuce patch.

Making "salad for one" does not have to be that great big bowl with a head of lettuce and eighty-seven chopped ingredients, which seems like too much food for one and way to much work. So here is where we redefine the "salad".

## sal·ad [**sal**-*uh*d]

*−noun*

1. A beautiful starter, main course or refreshing last course consisting of a few, really fresh ingredients and imagination. Dressed well.

So this description might sound more like a date than a plate and that is the idea. salad needs to be entertaining, exciting and mysterious. But, above all, for one to make it and eat it for one's self, it must be SIMPLE! There are recipes for salads in this chapter but once you get the hang of it you will make them with your own imagination. I will give you my ideas to start:

- Always dress the salad in a bowl and remove it onto the plate right away. Do not serve it or eat it in the bowl that dressed it. This is salad not soup.
- Limit the ingredients to two or three (there will be exceptions. After all, rules are meant to be broken)
- Always use fresh vegetables. If they are not right out of the ground fresh, skip it.
- Make your own dressing (which could be just a little olive oil or a squeeze of lemon.)

There are many salad dressings in the market. Find them because right next to them is where you are going to buy the ingredients that you need to make your own. Making dressing takes seconds and is WAY better. The bottled dressing in the store has crap in it.    If you will notice in the ideas on the previous page, nowhere does it say "pour crap on your salad".

Throughout this book I refer to Olive Oil. I always mean Extra Virgin Olive Oil. I never cook or dress salads with anything other than Extra Virgin. This is the pure olive oil with no other ingredients. Experiment and try different ones. The tastes are amazing and different. Some markets sell the smaller bottles. This is a great way to try several and not have them go bad, although I use so much of the stuff that I have yet to find a rancid bottle in my pantry.

Fennel, Blood Orange and Parmesan Salad

# FENNEL, BLOOD ORANGE AND PARMESAN

Q

I made this salad late one night for a new friend because the ingredients were the only things available at the all night market. She happened to be the manager of a pretty famous chef and I really did not want to disappoint her.


**INGREDIENTS**
**1 Fennel Bulb**
**2 Blood Oranges**
**Shaved Parmesan**

**TOOLS**
**Chef's knife (or mandolin)**
**Peeler**

**DRESSING**
**Extra Virgin Olive Oil and Aged Balsamic Vinegar**

1. Slice the fennel bulb into very thin pieces.

2. Separate the orange pieces then cut or tear in half.

3. Emulsify (whisk together) 2 tablespoons of olive oil and one teaspoon of balsamic in the bottom of a bowl.

4. Toss the fennel and oranges until well coated.


Place on plate and shave a few thin slices of cheese on top. Drizzle with a little of the left over dressing or just a drop or two of the straight balsamic.

# ROASTED CORN AND AGED GOAT CHEESE

This recipe is inspired by a dish I once had at Mario Batali's *ESCA* which is one of my favorite restaurants in New York.

**INGREDIENTS**
**1 Ear Roasted Corn**
**Aged Goat Cheese**
**Handful Chanterelle[1] Mushrooms, cut into pieces**
**A Few Leaves of Arugula**
**Walnuts**
**Butter**
**Olive Oil**

**TOOLS**
**Chef's Knife**
**Grill (optional)**
**Sauté Pan**

1. Roast the corn on the grill or in the oven. Make sure that you turn it often so it caramelizes nicely. Let it cool a bit.

2. In a pan, heat a pat of butter and tablespoon of olive oil.

3. Sauté the walnuts then add the Chanterelles (or other mushrooms if you can't get the chanterelles.)

4. Cut the corn off the cob.

---

1    Chanterelle Mushrooms are wonderful, woody mushrooms that tend to be quite expensive in most parts of the country. Keep an eye on the price and grab them when they are cheap. Remember, you only need a handful.

5. Toss corn, mushrooms, walnuts, and arugula with a little more olive oil. Do not over do the oil.

6. Grate the aged goat cheese over the salad. Make sure you get the <u>aged</u> goat cheese, as it is hard and can be grated.

A simple steak made complete by an Arugula and Fennel salad.

## ABOUT ARUGULA

I'm sure that you have heard that the darker the leafy vegetable, the better it is for you. The spicy, dark green leaf of the arugula (also known as, rocket, roquette, roqueta, rucula, rucola) fits into that category quite nicely. Fortunate for me, because I like it more than just about any other salad leaf. You will see it all over these pages. You can buy it in pre washed containers, or loose by the handful. There are a few different types. Baby arugula is the easiest as it generally tends to have smaller stems allowing it to go straight from the container into your bowl. If you are buying loose then wash and pat dry in paper towels, discarding all the larger stems.

# ARUGULA, FENNEL AND SHAVED PARMESAN

# Q

I had this salad for dinner one night with some sliced tomatoes drizzled with olive oil, salt and pepper.

## INGREDIENTS
**1 Fennel Bulb**
**Handful of Arugula**
**Shaved Parmesan**
**Olive Oil**
**Lemon**

## TOOLS
**Chef's knife (or mandolin)**
**Peeler (optional)**

1. Cut the top and bottom off the fennel bulb, saving a few of the frawns (The whispy, light green hairs sprouting out the top of the bulb) if there are any. You can finely chop them and add for a bit of color and freshness at the end.

2. Remove the toughest layer of the bulb. Stand the bulb up and thinly slice from the narrowest end. If you have a mandolin, this would be a good time to get it dirty.

3. Toss the fennel in a bowl with a handful of arugula.

4. Shave a good amount of parmesan. You want to end up with roughly equal parts arugula, parmesan and fennel, slightly less cheese if you prefer.

5. Drizzle a little olive oil and a squeeze of lemon. Toss so the leaves are very lightly coated with the oil.

6.  Remove to a plate and sprinkle with the chopped frawns and a little ground, black pepper. You shouldn't need any salt as the cheese will be slightly salty.

## How to cut a fennel bulb.

Remove the outer layer and slice in half.

Remove the hard center.

Using two angled cuts.

Slice lengthwise.

# BUTTER LETTUCE

Q

That is correct, this is a salad of one ingredient. The key here is to make this only when the lettuce looks REALLY good. I like to have this kind of a simple salad after a nice pasta or a meaty main course. Most Italians serve their salad after the main course. I don't really know how this works in the digestive process but I have never met an Italian, or an Italian meal that I didn't like. You never know, it might be because they eat their salad last.

## INGREDIENTS
**1 Head Butter Lettuce**
**Olive Oil**
**Champagne Vinegar**
**1 Shallot, minced**

## TOOLS
**Chef's knife**
**Whisk (optional)**

1. Thoroughly wash and dry the lettuce.

2. Tear or cut into pieces.

3. In a separate container, mix two parts olive oil to one part vinegar and add the minced shallot.

4. Whisk together to a single consistency. You can use a fork if you don't have a whisk.

5. Add a little salt and pepper to the dressing.

6. Lightly coat the leaves and serve right away.

A chef once told me that you can never make too much sauce, marinade or dressing. You can use too much, but you can never make too much. If you make extra, put it in a little container with a lid, refrigerate and use it tomorrow.

This salad can be made with any leaf that is fresh and good. The butter variety seems to me to be the most refreshing, but try everything. The vinaigrette (that is the little dressing you just whipped up) can have many variations as well. Try different kinds of vinegar. Red wine, white wine, raspberry. All work really well. You can also substitute the shallot with garlic, chives or basil. If you learn to do this quickly, you will have a great and satisfying meal and make your mom happy that you ate your greens.

## How to mince a shallot.

Cut off the ends and skin.

Slice thinly, lengthwise.

Group together.

Cut into little pieces.

  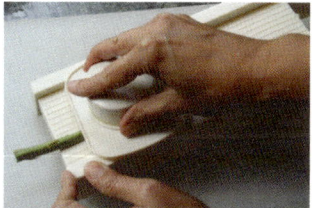

# MANDOLIN

I do not like to fill my cupboards with junk I will never use, but I do like to use this gadget called a mandolin. It is not because I am a musician, I just find that it makes the cutting of vegetables really simple. It is an inexpensive device (don't buy the expensive one), it's easy to clean and works really well.

# ASPARAGUS AND PARMESAN

## INGREDIENTS
**3-4 Big Pieces of Asparagus**
**Shaved Parmesan**
**Champagne Vinegar**
**1 Shallot, minced**
**Olive Oil**

## TOOLS
**Chef's knife (or mandolin)**
**Peeler (optional)**
**Medium Pan**

1.  Cut the very ends off of the asparagus.

2.  With a peeler, whittle the last couple of inches, exposing the white flesh.

3.  Soak the asparagus in ice-cold water for about 20 minutes.

4.  Put a pot full of water on to boil.

5.  When boiling, toss the asparagus in for about a minute.

6.  Remove and return to the ice water to stop the cooking.

7.  Remove from water and pat dry.

8.  With the mandolin, slice the asparagus length wise into thin spears and layer these spears with the shaved parmesan.

9.  Make the same vinaigrette from page 37.

# GRILLED VEGETABLE SALAD

I lived in Portland for a while and really learned to appreciate a sunny day to fire up the grill. The rest of the time I really appreciated the grill pan. I have a double and it is the best purchase I ever made. If you live somewhere that covers your grill in snow part of the year, this is a must. It sits over two burners on your stove, which means you can create a hot end, and works exactly the same as a grill, sans the mess.

This breaks the ingredient rule. But, unlike the other salads in this chapter, this is a meal. You can fix this as a starter or finisher but I often make this as my whole meal.

**INGREDIENTS**
**1 Red Pepper**
**1 Ear Corn**
**Portobello Mushroom**
**1 Red Onion**
**4-5 pieces Asparagus**
**Fresh Lettuce Leaves**
**Blue Cheese**
**Olive Oil**
**Aged Balsamic Vinegar**

**TOOLS**
**Grill or Grill Pan**
**Chef's Knife**

1. Start by grilling corn because it takes the most time.

2. Slice the onion and the pepper, but keep the asparagus and mushroom whole.

3. Drizzle all with olive oil

4. Grill until you are happy with them (15-20 Minutes).

5. Let the vegetables sit to cool.

6. Cut the corn off the cob,

7. Cut the vegetables into bite size chunks and toss all with the lettuce.

8. Crumple some blue cheese, drizzle with olive oil and some aged balsamic. Toss and enjoy.

**Slice peppers vertically, around the core.**

Variations on this will include your favorite and fresh vegetables of all sizes and shapes. Grilling vegetables brings out their sweetness without cooking out any of their essential vitamins and minerals. There really isn't a vegetable you can't grill, so experiment. You don't need to add the cheese or you can substitute goat cheese, feta, aged gouda or any other hard and/or crumbly cheese of your choice. I would avoid soft, runny cheeses, as they tend to be too messy for a salad. Have them after with a nice toasted baguette.

# GRILLED CAESAR SALAD

I know this sounds weird but just try it. You will be pleasantly surprised.

**INGREDIENTS**
**Romaine Lettuce**
**Grated Parmesan**
**Olive Oil**
**1 Lemon**
**Tin of Anchovies**
**Croutons**

**TOOLS**
**Chef's Knife**
**Grater**
**Grill or Grill Pan**

1. Drizzle the whole romaine head with olive oil and grill it, turning frequently. Alternatively, you can break the leaves off and grill them individually. Either way, they only need to be on the grill for a minute or two at the most.

2. In a salad bowl, squeeze the juice of one lemon; add twice as much olive oil.

3. Crush two or three anchovy fillets into the liquid and let dissolve. If you do not like anchovies substitute 2 tablespoons Worcestershire sauce.

4. Finely grate about a quarter cup of parmesan.

5. Mix all together then toss with the romaine and a handful of croutons. Shave some more parmesan on top.

# TOMATOES

Tomatoes are the one vegetable (actually they are a fruit) that people either love or they hate. My wife hates broccoli, but then again it's hard to find many people that LOVE broccoli. The same holds true with Brussels sprouts, lima beans and squash. Just about any vegetable that our moms ruined when we were children is subject to this sort of outdated emotional reaction.

Mom, on the other hand, rarely ruined tomatoes. I remember them sliced at every meal in the summer with only a little salt added. I remember picking them from the plants in the backyard. I remember buying them at farm stands or in some farmer's driveway, or from the back of a pick up truck. Tomatoes were the most flavorful, stand alone food of summer.

Today, tomatoes are a bit of a challenge. Unless you grow them - or you have a neighbor that grows them - finding a nice, tasty, ripe tomato is really hard. The reason is quite simple. Unlike most other plants, tomatoes have to ripen COMPLETELY on the vine. If they are picked when they are the slightest bit green they will not become that sweet, acidic orange globe from our memory. They will ripen, that is, they will continue to turn color and become softer but the flavor will not grow once they are picked.

So the problem is that stores cannot buy ripe tomatoes, drive them across the state or the country and expect them to be anything other than rotten. So, needless to say, one needs to go out of one's way to get a great, ripe tomato.

In my humble opinion, it is worth every minute and every mile. So my suggestions are the following: go out to the country farm stand, go to the farmers market, grow them yourself or if all else fails, try the ones at the best produce section you can find. For the most part, stay away from roma's and giant ones grown in hot houses. The heirlooms can sometimes be flavorful. You will just have to try them out.

# Q SLICED TOMATOES

I know you really don't need a recipe for sliced tomatoes. It's just that some people forget that one of the very best ways to eat a delicious, ripe tomato is simply sliced. If the skin bothers you then peel them as well. I like them au natural.

You can dress them up with any or all of the following:

Sprinkle of salt
Twist of pepper
Drizzle of good olive oil
Chiffonade of basil
A few drops of balsamic vinegar

Chiffonade basil by rolling leaves together and slicing.

# TOMATO SALAD

Q

It's worth repeating: If you can't find fresh, great tasting tomatoes, don't bother.

## INGREDIENTS
**1- 2 Ripe Tomatoes, roughly chopped**
**1/4 of a Red Onion, roughly chopped**
**1 Clove of Garlic, minced**
**1 Teaspoon Fresh Basil, roughly chopped (or chiffonade)**
**2 Tablespoons Good Olive Oil**
**1 Teaspoon Balsamic Vinegar (as good as you can afford)**
**Salt and Pepper**

## TOOLS
**Chef's knife**

1. Chop all of the ingredients

2. Toss in a bowl with the olive oil.

3. Carefully add the balsamic vinegar. The actual amount of vinegar you add will depend on how strong and sweet it is.

4. Salt and Pepper liberally.

### RED ONION TIP

If the onion is nice and fresh then it will not over power the tomatoes. If, on the other hand, it knocks you down when you cut into it, use a lot less. Uncooked onions are delicious but a little goes a very long way. And, if you make this for company, make sure you both eat some.

# TOMATO BREAD SALAD

This is the perfect summer salad to make with some left over, home baked, day old bread. Unlike processed bread, when you either bake or buy home baked type bread (ala LaBrea Bakery), it only lasts a few days.

## INGREDIENTS
**2 Slices Day Old Bread, torn into chunks**
**1- 2 Ripe Tomatoes, roughly chopped**
**1/4 of a Red Onion, roughly chopped**
**1 Clove Garlic, minced**
**1 Teaspoon of Fresh Basil, roughly chopped (or chiffonade)**
**3 Tablespoons Good Olive Oil**
**1 Tablespoon Red Wine Vinegar**
**Salt and Pepper**

## TOOLS
**Chef's Knife**

1. Tear the bread into bite size chunks into a bowl.

2. Salt and Pepper the bread.

3. Peal and slice the tomatoes over the bread, so the juices of the tomatoes cover and coat the bread.

4. Let the tomatoes and bread sit for about an hour to thoroughly soak the bread.

5. Toss the onion, garlic, basil, olive oil and vinegar into the tomato and bread mixture. Salt and Pepper to taste.

# Chapter 5
# MEAT & CHICKEN

I eat meat. I have attempted vegetarianism from time to time. I go through spurts where I mainly eat fruits and vegetables, but my body needs protein and I have never conquered the process of achieving that without the help of my butcher.

Further, I like a good steak occasionally, but I try not to eat red meat very much. Having said that, the easiest and most successful way to shop and cook for one is to go to the market, choose a protein, a vegetable to accompany it and a bottle of wine to wash it down. So, if you enjoy meat and chicken: tuck in!

# ONE PAN CHICKEN #1

This is a one pan chicken dish, of which there are many variations and should become a staple for you, since it is quick and clean up is a breeze. If you would like rice you will have to clean a second pan.

## INGREDIENTS
**Chicken Thighs – 2, 3 or 4 depending on the package**
**1 Small White Onion, roughly chopped**
**Handful of Mushrooms, chopped**
**Chicken Broth**
**2 Baby Bok Choy (could be any other green veg)**
**Lemon**
**Thyme**
**Rice**

## TOOLS
**Chef's knife**
**Med. Sauté Pan**
**Small Sauce Pan**

1. Wash and pat dry the chicken.

2. In a sauce pan, put the rice on per instructions on package.

3. Squeeze the lemon over the chicken, season with salt, pepper.

4. Peal the leaves of the stems of the thyme and sprinkle over the chicken.

5. Prep a sauté pan with 2 teaspoons olive oil and one pat of butter over medium heat.

6. Brown the chicken, skin side down.

7. Turn over and add onions and mushrooms.

8. Sauté for a few minutes.

9. Add enough chicken broth to cover chicken half way.

10. Cover and simmer for about 10 minutes.

11. Add bok choy and simmer for another 10 minutes.

12. As the rice cooks, reduce the liquid in the chicken pan by uncovering and turning up the heat.

Serve two chicken thighs over the rice and spoon on the mushroom, onion and bok choy with some of the left over juices.

## RICE

Cooking rice is dead simple. Buy rice and read the package. Usually it's one cup of rice and two cups of water. Bring to a boil and then turn to simmer for 15 minutes, stirring as directed. My son has been making rice since he was 6. You can do it.

#  ONE PAN CHICKEN #2

While working on a project in New York recently, I had an opportunity to cook a lot for myself. The fee on the project was not huge so I was on a tight budget. One night, I went to the market with the challenge of spending the cash in my pocket to make myself dinner. I had about nine dollars.

There is a wonderful little market in my neighborhood that is not huge but has just about everything that one would need. I first went to the meat department and found a package of three chicken thighs (organic) for $3.20. I went back to the produce section and got a white onion and a handful of white mushrooms (the other mushroom options were just too expensive). I also got a small amount of arugula, knowing that I had some wonderful parmesan at the apartment and could complement my chicken with a nice salad.

## INGREDIENTS
3 Chicken Thighs
1 Small White Onion, diced
Handful of White Mushrooms, chopped
3 Cloves of Garlic, minced
Tablespoon Olive Oil
Splash of White Wine

## TOOLS
Sauté pan
Chef's knife

1. Sauté the garlic and onion in the olive oil.

2. Add the mushrooms and continue to sauté.

3. After a minute or two, wedge in the chicken thighs to the bottom of the pan.

4. Turn the chicken occasionally and stir the onions and mushrooms so they don't burn.

5. After 10 minutes add the wine and cook off the alcohol. This only takes a few minutes.

6. By the time you reduce the wine by half the alcohol should have nearly evaporated. Lower the heat and cover until the chicken is cooked. This should take about another 10 minutes.

7. Serve the chicken smothered in the onions and mushrooms. You will love this dish. The onions make it sweet and delicious.

Finish your meal with a refreshing arugula and parmesan salad.

# Q CHICKEN THIGHS FOR NOAH

If you haven't noticed yet, the chicken dishes in this section are similar. Please cook all three of these dishes and notice how the small changes can make a big difference. Also imagine what you might do to the basic concept to make it your own. The reason that I say package of thighs is that I first made this for my stepson Noah and myself and that was what we found at the store. I didn't have much money and a package of thighs that looked good was only three dollars. It looked like 4 thighs but it turned out to be 6. It doesn't really matter, as you will gladly eat these as leftovers.

## INGREDIENTS
Package Of Chicken Thighs
1 Red Pepper (Chopped)
1 Onion (Chopped)
2 Cloves of Garlic
1 Cup of Sliced Mushrooms (Buy the presliced ones if available)
1 Cup Chicken Broth
Tablespoon Chopped Rosemary
Glug of Cream or Half And Half (Optional)
2 Tablespoons Olive Oil
Salt And Pepper

## TOOLS
Large Sauté Pan With Cover
Chefs Knife
Slotted Spoon

1.  Chop the onion, garlic and pepper.

2.  Heat the olive oil and sauté the vegetables.

3.  Cook until the onion is translucent.

4.  Salt and pepper the chicken and add it to the pan.

5.  Pour the mushrooms on top of the chicken. They will work themselves into the broth created by the chicken.

6.  Cook on each side for about 5 minutes.

7.  Add the chicken broth and bring to a boil.

8.  Turn to a simmer and cover, leaving the lid cracked to let some of the liquid evaporate.

9.  Cook for about 20 minutes.

10. Remove chicken to a serving plate and cover with the strained vegetables.

11. Add the rosemary and bring the remaining broth to a boil to reduce by half.

12. Turn the flame off and stir in the cream.

13. Strain or just pour over the chicken.

# Q STUFFED PORK CHOPS

This is truly a fast and easy meal. This dish requires only one sauté pan but make sure it is approved to go in the oven.

### INGREDIENTS
**2 Good Size Pork Chops (can be on the bone)**
**Handful of Spinach**
**Goat Cheese or other mild cheese**
**Olive Oil**
**Salt and Pepper**
**Minced Garlic (optional)**
**Lemon**

### TOOLS
**Chef's knife**
**Sauté Pan**

1. Pre heat oven to 350º

2. Thoroughly wash the spinach (a bunch of raw spinach, unwashed, is about a third of the price of packaged).

3. Soak it in iced cold water for about 10 minutes.

4. Dry with paper towels.

5. Sauté the spinach with the garlic in a little olive oil until the spinach is wilted.

6. While the spinach is sautéing, wash and pat dry the pork chops.

7. When the spinach is cooked (about 5 minutes) set aside in a bowl. If you have never cooked spinach before, don't freak out. It will reduce to about 1/5$^{th}$ the amount. You can also leave out the garlic if you wish. I didn't use the garlic the first time I tried this because I thought there might be kissing involved in the later part of the evening.

8. Cut a slit nearly all the way through the pork chop, essentially butterflying them.

9. Salt and pepper both sides.

10. Stuff a little of the cheese, a little of the spinach, a little more cheese, etc until there is a consistent layer of stuffing (not too much.)

11. Pour off any excess liquid from the pan and add another splash of olive oil.

12. Pan-fry the chops, browning both sides.

13. Stick the pan in the oven and finish by baking for about ten minutes, depending on the thickness of the chop. WARNING: Be careful after you remove the pan, as it will remain hot for quite some time. My son suggests a "hot pan" sign. I grabbed the handle of a pan fresh out of the oven once. I will swear to you this is something you only do once!

Try stuffing with apples or pear or fennel frawns. Anything slightly sweet and not too strong. I once tried this with Stilton cheese and it completely overwhelmed the chop.

# Q BLADE LAMB CHOP WITH BROCCOLINI

Sometimes it's either late or you don't want a huge meal. This is one of those fulfilling meals that is simple, quick and contains no carbs. Always a good idea. You could fix a second veg or a salad if you want to make more food. If you make this just as it is you will not be going hungry.

## INGREDIENTS
**1 Blade Lamb Chop**
**1 Bunch Broccolini (Aka Asparation or Baby Broccoli)**
**1 Lemon**
**1 Clove Garlic, Minced**
**Fresh Rosemary**
**Dried Chili Flakes**

## TOOLS
**Non-Stick Pan**
**Sauté Pan**
**Cutting Board**
**Chef's Knife**

The Blade chop is a great find. You may not find it in every market but usually it is a lot less than the other lamb and every bit as tasty. It has a large bone and is therefore cheaper. If you can't find this cut you can always substitute two or three regular lamb chops or one large chop.

1. Marinate the chop with a little olive oil, lemon juice, salt and pepper and finely chopped rosemary. You don't need for it to marinate for more than a few minutes.

2. Heat a non-stick pan. You do not need any fat in the pan to cook this meat.

3. Cook one side of the chop until quite brown. Turn.

4. Chop the stems off of the broccolini. If you really still only have one pan you can cook the whole meal in it but I suggest that you use two.

5. Heat 2 teaspoons of olive oil in a sauté pan.

6. Add a pinch of red chilli flakes and the garlic.

7. Simmer on low heat for a few minutes.

8. Add the broccolini and salt and pepper it.

9. You might need to sprinkle in a bit more olive oil.

10. Sauté for about 5 minutes until it is bright green but still crunchy.

**LAMB WARNING**

If you live in an apartment like I did when I first cooked this, make sure that you have a good fan. Lamb lingers.

11. Cook the other side of the chop until it is done the way you like it. For me, a one inch thick chop usually takes about 15 minutes.

12. Add a tablespoon of balsamic vinegar to the broccolini and cook down. About another minute.

Enjoy this with a nice Pinot Noir or a glass of Syrah.

# LAMB SHANK

I think that most of you will want to cook this on a Saturday or Sunday or on one of those days that you have a cold and just really didn't feel like going to work. Mainly because it takes some time to cook. The prep is easy. The dish is absolutely delicious and is perfect for a cold winter night. Oh, and if you think you caught me cheating, yes there is another lamb shank recipe later in the book in the date night chapter. It is slightly different.

## INGREDIENTS
1 Lamb Shank
1 Carrot
1 Small Onion
2 Celery Stalks
1 Medium Potato
3 Cloves Garlic
1/2 Cup Red Wine
1/2 Cup Water or Broth (Vegetable or Chicken)
Fresh Thyme
Fresh Rosemary

## TOOLS
Dutch Oven or Heavy Oven-Proof Pan with a lid
Cutting board
Chef's knife

1.  Pre heat the oven to 350º.

2.  Chop all the vegetables into bite size pieces.

3.  Sliver the garlic. (Cut lengthwise into thin pieces)

4.  Sauté the onion, celery and carrot until the onion is translucent.

5.  Remove vegetables from the pan to a bowl or plate.

6.  Trim any excess fat from the shank.

7.  Rub it with a bit of olive oil, cut a few slits in the top and slip the garlic in. Salt and pepper.

8.  Brown in the same pan.

9.  Once browned, cover with the vegetables and potatoes.

10. Salt and pepper the vegetables, pour the wine and broth over and add the herbs.

11. Cover and cook in the oven for 2 hours, or until the shank is tender. Check for liquid and tenderness after about an hour or so.

This is your whole meal in this little dutch oven. I have a small one that is perfect for one lamb shank.

# STIR FRY VEGETABLES AND CHICKEN, OR...

This is the first dish that I learned to cook when I was in college (unless you count hamburger helper). The great gift of this recipe is that produce is available in whatever amount you would like to purchase.

I say "or..." because you can make this dish as is or leave out the chicken or add some shrimp or steak or anything that you have or want.

This recipe is more of a lesson than a dish. There are many variations and once you are comfortable with the process, you can feed yourself many nights by improvising and having fun.

## INGREDIENTS
**1 Boneless, Skinless Chicken Breast**
**Small Stock Broccoli Or Broccolini**
**1 Bunch Of Green Onions**
**3 Cloves Of Garlic, minced**
**1 Apple, cored and chopped**
**Small Handful of Snow Peas, de-stemmed**
**1 Red Pepper, chopped**
**Small Handful Of Mushrooms, chopped**
**Little Piece Of Fresh Ginger, minced**
**2 Tablespoons Vegetable Oil or Olive Oil**
**Soy Sauce**
**Rice**

## TOOLS
**Wok or Large Sauté Pan**
**Wooden Spoon**
**Chef's Knife**

1. Cut the chicken into bite size chunks. Make sure to use a different chopping board and a different knife and wash your knife and your hands after you prepare the chicken.

2. Chop all of the vegetables into bite sized pieces.

3. Start the rice of your choice now.

4. Heat the oil (I prefer olive oil but it does add a taste that some don't like with the other ingredients)

5. Sauté the garlic and ginger over medium heat, being careful not to burn it.

6. Add the chicken in the oil, Salt and pepper, careful to not use too much salt.

7. Once the chicken is thoroughly cooked, which should only take a few minutes, either slide it up the side of the wok or remove it from the pan.

8. Add the vegetables and a little more oil if needed.

9. Add the vegetables in order of their texture, the harder ones first. Onion, pepper, broccoli for a few minutes, then the apple, mushrooms, etc. Please do not over cook the vegetables. Salt and Pepper the vegetables as you go. They want to be vibrant in their color and still retain a little crunch.

10. Add the chicken back, drizzle with soy sauce and cook together for a few more minutes.

Serve over rice or pasta or nothing at all.

# VEGETABLES

There are several vegetable recipes in this book, usually included in other recipes. Regardless of your protein choice (Fish, chicken, meat, etc) an accompanying vegetable balances out the meal. Just about every vegetable can be prepared quickly and easily one of the following ways. Buy what is fresh, in season and what you like.

Brussels Sprouts and Squash.

## ROASTING
Cut into bite sized pieces and place in an oven-proof container, drizzle with olive oil, salt and pepper and cook in a 350 degree oven until tender. It usually takes between 30-45 minutes.

Grilled corn on the cob.

## GRILLING
Grill whole or cut into large enough pieces so as to not fall through the grill. Drizzle with a little olive oil or plain with a little salt and pepper. The fire brings out the flavor.

Snow Peas and Leeks.

## SAUTÉING
Cut into bite sized pieces and heat in a pan over fairly high heat with some sort of fat: butter, olive oil, etc. Keep them moving so they don't burn. What could be better than hot vegetables in butter?

# Chapter 6
## SEAFOOD

One of the big challenges of cooking for one's self is that markets conspire against us. Everything is boxed or packaged for more than one serving and even the butcher gives you a discount on quantity. Not usually so with seafood.

You can (and should) buy just what you need right before you need it. Fresh seafood is the delight of all delights in my humble opinion. It is also very quick and easy to prepare. In fact, whenever I have tried to make it the least bit complicated I have had a disaster. That is the reason why you will not find Potato Crusted Halibut in this book.

There is no question that seafood is expensive. Buy only what you will eat. With the possible exception of salmon, it's not really good leftovers anyway. Seafood is also very good for you so don't feel bad splurging every now and then.

There are a few considerations when buying seafood. Most good supermarkets and dedicated seafood stores let you know where the fish come from, if they were farm raised or caught wild and if they have been frozen. Don't be automatically turned off by fish that has been frozen. Most frozen fish is frozen at sea very nearly after it is caught. You probably won't have any fish any fresher than a fish that was frozen at sea.

I prefer mostly wild caught although there are some farm raised salmon that are as delicious as wild caught North Atlantic. Use your eyes and nose and do some experimenting. Unless you have a particular allergy, almost all seafood is great. Like most things in life, don't be afraid to ask questions. Even in the most modest markets I have found really knowledgeable staff behind the fish counter.

Preparing a meal with seafood is very simple. It is the star. Accompany it with something simple: Plain pasta or rice, a simple salad or grilled vegetables.

## GRILLING

Not everyone lives in sunny Southern California (although it sure seems like it when you are sitting in the parking lot called the 405 freeway). You need to find some way of grilling. Grilling is an easy, clean and efficient way of cooking just about every food. I've even grilled pizza. There are grills of all sizes and prices. There are indoor grills, outdoor grills, propane, gas, electric and charcoal. And some combinations of all.

You should choose based on your locale, temperament and space. I do live in Southern California and have a propane grill. Whatever you choose, make it easy on yourself. If you live in Maine and don't want to wear a coat while cooking, there are beautiful, indoor electric grills that are easy to clean. I have one for rainy days. Stove Top Grill Pans are another great indoor alternative.

# GRILLED SEA SCALLOPS

There are several types and sizes of scallops. When in doubt, ask your fishmonger which are tastiest that day. I usually prefer the larger sea scallops or the really tasty and expensive diver scallops. Diver scallops are sea scallops that are hand picked by divers. They tend to be bigger and really good and good for the environment.

## INGREDIENTS
**3 Large Sea Scallops (or as many as you can eat and afford)**
**1 Lemon**
**Salt And Pepper**
**Olive Oil**

## TOOLS
**Grill or Grill Pan**
**Tongs or fork for turning**

1. Lightly drizzle olive oil and a nice squeeze of lemon juice over the washed scallops.

2. Lightly salt (with sea salt or Fleur de sel) and pepper.

3. Let sit to marinate for 15 or 20 minutes. Not long.

4. Heat the grill to a pretty high temperature.

5. Grill the scallops for about 3 - 5 minutes on each side. Even really large ones don't take long to cook.

Serve with a little more lemon juice drizzled over them.

Since you have the grill on you might also want to grill a vegetable to accompany the scallops. A grilled vegetable salad or the grilled romaine are two great salads that go well with the scallops (see Salad Chapter).

I often eat them with nothing else. As an alternative, scallops are great on a fettuccini or linguini. Fresh pasta is perfect if you can find it. Continue the theme of the scallops, toss with the pasta and just drizzle a little really fresh, young olive oil and some fleur de sel.

# GRILLED SHRIMP

Q

Shrimp are a pain in the ass. They have tails and veins running down their backs and are, well, shrimpy. BUT, always check your fishmonger for the one way that makes sense for a single person with not a lot of patience. That is, the medium to large, de-veined with tails removed, uncooked shrimp (or prawn, if you must). Suddenly, cooking shrimp is easy, delicious and quick! If you find the de-veined that still has the tail it is not the end of the world. The tail comes off quite easily when uncooked. All you do is grab it with your thumb and forefinger and squeeze.

## INGREDIENTS
**6 – 8 (or as many as you can eat) Medium, de-veined, uncooked Shrimp**
**(NOTE: Eating pre-cooked shrimp is like chewing on rubber.)**
**1 Lemon**
**Salt and Pepper**
**Olive Oil**

## TOOLS
**Grill**
**Tongs or fork for turning**

1. Lightly drizzle olive oil and a nice squeeze of lemon juice over the washed shrimps.

2. Lightly salt (with sea salt or Fleur de sel) and pepper. Is this starting to sound familiar?

3. Let sit to marinate for about 15-20 minutes. If you let either the shrimp or scallops sit longer you will be cooking them in the acid of the lemon. It's a nice dish called ceviche, but not what we are after.

4. Grill for 2-3 minutes and turn. Don't cook them too long or they become rubbery. Shrimp are really easy to cook as they turn white and orange. As soon as they turn color they are done.

The same advice applies as it did with the scallops. Pasta, salad, etc.

Also, if you are having company, the combination of grilled shrimp and grilled scallops makes both culinary and financial sense. This is not in the Date Night chapter but it could be. Everyone enjoys simply prepared, fresh seafood.

Grilled asparagus on a double grill pan. Simple and delicious.

# HALIBUT WRAPPED IN FOIL

This works with all kinds of flaky, tender white fish. I happen to love the taste of Halibut and it is widely available. If it is too expensive then try Cod or Dover Sole.

**INGREDIENTS**
**1/4lb Halibut (or Sole, Monkfish, Swordfish, etc.)**
**1 Lemon**
**1 Shallot, Minced**
**1 Teaspoon Fresh Thyme, Chopped**
**1 Teaspoon Minced Fresh Ginger (Or 1/2 Teaspoon Ground, Dried Ginger)**
**Salt And Pepper**
**Olive Oil**

**TOOLS**
**Grill**
**Aluminium foil**
**Chef's knife**

You can buy fresh ginger everywhere and it comes in various sizes. Buy a little piece. It is very inexpensive and a completely different taste than the dried variety. If, for some reason you can't find fresh or you just forgot, then the dried will be fine.

1.  Pre-heat the grill then knock the coals down, or turn down the flame to medium low. This is more baking than grilling. You can also do this in the oven.

2.  Make a pouch out of a large piece of aluminium foil by doubling over once and forming a boat.

3.  Place the fish in the bottom of the boat, drizzle it with the oil and lemon, sprinkle the garlic, ginger and thyme.

4.  Very lightly salt and pepper.

5.  Close the pouch by bringing the long ends together over the fish and folding them together twice, then fold the short ends. This should keep the liquids sealed in during cooking.

6.  Place the pouch on the cooler end of the grill (if there is such a thing) and cook for about 15-20 minutes, or about 10 minutes per 1/2" of thickness. You do not need to turn as the fish is actually poaching in the lemon, oil and it's own liquid.

# How To Mince Ginger
### Demonstrated by Noah, age 13

Start by cutting off the skin.

Clean a good sized chunk.

Cut into slivers.

Cut in the opposite direction to mince.

## GRILLED SALMON

My friend Steve grew up in Scotland, but hated fish. That is, until one evening, when we talked him into tasting a wild caught Scottish salmon. I must admit, it was the best fish I had ever eaten and for Steve it was immediate conversion. Now he eats all seafood including sushi.

Salmon is readily available, not too expensive and incredibly good for you. It is a meaty fish and tends not to be to "fishy". I don't like it too adulterated. It has tons of flavor all on it's own.

**INGREDIENTS**
**Fillet of Salmon with the skin on (if possible)**
**1 Lemon**
**1 Teaspoon Minced Fresh Ginger (optional)**
**Salt And Pepper**
**Olive Oil**

**TOOLS**
**Grill**
**Spatula**
**Chefs Knife**
**Cutting Board**
**Tweezers or clean Needle Nose Pliers (optional)**

I used to have a fishmonger near me when I lived in Boston who would promise to give me my money back if I found any bones. The truth is, sometimes they don't get all of them when cleaning and filleting a fish. So, run your fingers over the fillet and check for bones.
A pair of tweezers or clean needle nosed pliers work great for gently removing any leftover bones. Try not to destroy the flesh of the fish while removing them.

1. Rub a little olive oil onto the fish. Not too much as the fish is already a bit oily.

2. Squeeze the lemon over it

3. Salt and pepper and add the ginger. The ginger is really optional. I have tried many additions to salmon and come back to ginger or nothing at all.

4. Place the salmon skin side down on a hot grill and cover. Do not turn. It should take between 15-20 minutes. The first time you cook salmon you might want to make a small cut in the thickest part to see if it is cooked to your liking. The thickness, the amount of heat and your definition of done all contribute to the length of time it takes.

Rice, a baked potato, simple pasta, or just a salad would all be perfect sides to round out this delicious meal.

# Q  SAUTÉED SCALLOPS

<u>INGREDIENTS</u>
3-5 Sea Scallops (depending on the size, your appetite and budget)
1 Lemon
Really Good Sea Salt
Pepper
2 Pats Really Good Butter
Olive Oil
Aged Balsamic Vinegar

<u>TOOLS</u>
Sauté Pan
Tongs

1. Sit the scallops on a plate and let them get to room temperature.

2. Squeeze the juice of one lemon over the scallops, drizzle with olive oil then salt and pepper.

3. Let sit for 10-20 minutes. Not long, as we talked about before. You don't want the lemon to cook them.

4. Melt the butter in the sauté pan over medium heat.

5. Add the scallops and cook for five minutes on each side, covering when cooking the first side.

6. Add about 2 tablespoons of balsamic vinegar (less if it is very old) to the pan and let it thicken. About another minute.

The older the balsamic the sweeter it becomes, so you will have to judge exactly how much you use based on the sweetness. Don't let the vinegar overpower the scallops.

This is really nice over lemon risotto or with a simple salad. I have a hard time convincing my wife to eat scallops with anything other than a salad, and even that she goes for begrudgingly.

## SAUTÉ

Sautéing is essentially pan-frying, quickly - on hi heat. Seafood is perfect for the sauté pan. Even thick cuts of tuna can be enjoyed just briefly seared, remaining essentially raw in the middle. The biggest consideration when sautéing seafood is in what sort of fat you will cook. Often, the seafood will take on some of the taste of the fat. This is not a bad thing as long as you choose wisely. After all, the heal of my shoe would taste good sautéd in enough butter. But, butter is not always a great choice. Unless you use clarified butter, butter tends to burn at pretty low temperatures. Olive oil is often a great choice. Probably because the Italians, who live by the coast have been preparing the simplest and most delicious seafood for hundreds of years and the combination of seafood and olive oil is naturally symbiotic.

# SEARED TUNA OVER SALAD

Quite frankly, I have been intimidated by tuna most of my cooking life. Mainly because when I finally did get the nerve up to buy it and cook it I screwed it up. But, like most mistakes in the kitchen, I was trying to make it too complicated and was applying rules for other fish. For some reason, I always thought it had to be cooked all the way through for it to be good. What I always forgot was that I had eaten tuna at sushi restaurants for as long as I can remember. Why should it be any different at home.

So the key is to buy REALLY fresh and good tuna. If you come across some with that really deep red color then buy it. Don't bother if you are not completely convinced that it is wonderful, sushi grade tuna.

## INGREDIENTS
**1 Hunk of Tuna**
**1 Lemon**
**Really good Sea Salt**
**Pepper**
**Olive Oil**
**Butter**
**White Wine**
**Salad Greens**
**½ Teaspoon Ground Ginger**

## TOOLS
**Sauté Pan**
**Tongs**

1. Squeeze the lemon over the tuna. Salt and pepper.

2. Heat the oil in a sauté pan.

3. Sear all sides of the tuna for no more than 3 minutes a side. The center will be raw.

4. When the tuna is seared on all sides sit it on a plate of salad greens.

5. Add a pat of butter, another squeeze of lemon and about 1/2 cup wine to the pan.

6. Turn up the heat to reduce the wine by half, scraping any bits off the bottom of the pan and add the ginger.

Pour this dressing/sauce over the tuna and salad.

# Q SEARED SALMON AND AVOCADO QUESADILLA

## INGREDIENTS
**Salmon Fillet**
**Avocado**
**Mild Chedder Cheese, shredded**
**Salsa**
**2 Tortillas**
**Olive Oil**

## TOOLS
**Sauté Pan (non-stick)**
**Chef's Knife**

1. In a non-stick pan heat a teaspoon of olive oil. You really do not need much.

2. Salt and Pepper both sides of the Salmon. Either buy a small piece of salmon for this or plan to make more than one. You can use left over salmon for this dish if you have some.

3. Over fairly high heat, drop the salmon in the oil. Let it sear on one side for a few minutes, turn and repeat. The idea is that you are just cooking the outer sides of the salmon, leaving the inside practically raw. If you prefer salmon cooked through then leave it on longer.

4. Remove the salmon to a paper towel and let sit for a few minutes.

5. When it cools a little, slice it or break it into bite size chunks.

6. If you are fastidious, wipe the pan with a towel and add another drop of oil. I sometimes use spray olive oil for this process.

7. Cook one side of one of the tortillas for a minute and then remove.

8. Cook the other tortilla on both sides.

9. After you flip the second tortilla, sprinkle the cheese and salmon.

10. Cover with the first tortilla, cooked side down.

11. Flip the whole thing after a couple of minutes. If you are brave you can do this with a flick of the wrist. If not, use a large spatula for assistance.

12. Cook for another minute and remove from the pan. The whole thing should slide off onto a plate.

## TORTILLAS

Depending on where you live, you may or may not be well versed in this flat, round Mexican version of bread. There are a few types: flour, corn, pre-cooked and uncooked. They all amount to a round wrapper to fill with great stuff.

My personal favorite is the uncooked flour tortilla. Unlike their pre-cooked brothers, uncooked ones are usually found in the refrigerated deli section of the supermarket. They are also slightly harder to find outside of the border states, so you might have to buy the pre-cooked ones. The uncooked tortillas can be cooked in about one minute in the bottom of a sauté pan, a grill, a griddle or directly on top of a stove burner.

13. Peel back the tortilla and arrange slices of avocado and salsa.

14. Cut into wedges and serve with a little more salsa.

# SPICY SCALLOPS AND FRESH PASTA

This may seem similar to the sautéed scallops, but these have a completely different taste. Once you have cooked this once or twice you might consider doubling it and inviting over a friend. This might seem like a lot of ingredients and sound complicated, but it is actually quite easy and really hard to screw up.

## INGREDIENTS
**3-5 Sea Scallops (5 medium or 3 Large)**
**1 Lemon**
**1 Teaspoon Lemon Zest From That Lemon**
**1 Small Shallot, minced**
**1 Thin Slice Prosciutto, cubed**
**Really Good Sea Salt**
**Pepper**
**2 pats Really Good Butter**
**Olive Oil**
**Package Fresh Linguini or Spaghetti**
**1 Teaspoon Red Pepper Flakes**
**Splash Of White Wine**
**Pinch Of Fresh Thyme**
**Italian Parsley, roughly chopped**
**Parmesan**

## TOOLS
**Sauté Pan**
**Large Pot**
**Tongs**
**Fine Grater**
**Chef's Knife**

1. Fill the large pot with water and salt generously. Turn the flame on high.

2. Wash the scallops and place them into a shallow bowl or plate.

3. Salt, pepper and squeeze the juice from half a lemon and let them sit.

4. Mince the Shallot.

5. Cube the prosciutto. You want the prosciutto to end up being little flakes so cut it to about ¼" squares.

6. Warm about 3 tablespoons of olive oil in a sauté pan over medium low heat.

7. Sauté the prosciutto until it starts to get a little bit crispy.

8. Add the shallots, red pepper flakes and a pat of butter. Be careful not to burn the shallots.

9. Grate about a teaspoon of lemon zest into the pan.

10. Add the thyme, pinching off little bits from the stems. A little thyme goes a long way in this dish.

11. Gently sauté all of these ingredients together for a few minutes.

12. Once the water barely starts to boil put the scallops into the pan.

13. Cook on one side for about 5 minutes.

14. Turn the scallops and add a glug of white wine.

15. Sauté on the other side for 5 minutes.

16. Remove the scallops from the pan onto a plate.

17. Add another pat of butter to the pan and the rest of the lemon zest.

18. Turn the heat up a little to reduce the wine if it has not already.

19. The water should be boiling. Put a good handful of the fresh pasta into the water and stir.

20. Take this time to rough chop the parsley.

21. The pasta should be cooked. Fresh pasta only takes a few minutes. Remove it from the water.

22. Add the pasta to the pan and turn the heat off.

23. Coat the pasta thoroughly with the sauce.

24. Grate a little parmesan over it.

25. Add the scallops back to the pan.

Plate the pasta and scallops; grate a bit more cheese and sprinkle with the chopped parsley. You will want to kiss me on the lips after you take your first bite, I promise.

# CLAMS AND SPAGHETTI

My friend Steve McLaughlin (the same guy that used to not eat seafood) makes a dish similar to this every Thursday for his staff and whoever else gathers at his studio for lunch. Whenever I am in London I try not to miss it, even if I am not working on a project with him.

Making clams for yourself may seem like a big production and not worth it. This could not be further from the truth. Clams are really quick and easy to make and as we have discussed before, pasta is just boiling water.

## INGREDIENTS
6-10 Med Size Clams (buy just as many as you can eat)
Handful of Spaghetti
1 Thick Piece of Pancetta, chopped into smallish cubes (1/4" or so) About ¼ Cup
2 Cloves Garlic, Minced
Tablespoon Olive Oil
Teaspoon Red Pepper Flakes
½ Cup White Wine
Glug of Sambuca
Chopped Italian Parsley

## TOOLS
Large Sauce Pan
Sauté Pan w/lid
Chef's Knife
Cutting Board
Large Bowl
Colander
Tongs

The only time consuming aspect of cooking this dish is cleaning the clams. This doesn't actually take much time but they need to soak for a while to make sure all of the sand and silt is removed. If you have a colander that will fit inside a large bowl then use those for this process.

1. Rinse and soak the clams in enough cold water to cover. Let them sit for 10-20 minutes

2. Pour out the dirty water and repeat 2 or three times until there is hardly any dirt left in the bottom of the bowl.

3. Put enough water in a pan to cook the pasta, generously salt and boil water.

4. When the water boils, add the pasta.

5. In the sauté pan heat the olive oil.

6. Add the pancetta and sauté over med heat (about 5 minutes).

7. Add garlic and red pepper flakes. Sauté for a few minutes.

8. Add wine and Sambuca and turn the heat to high.

9. When the liquid begins to steam add the clams and cover. It only takes a couple of minutes to steam the clams.

10. Check on them after the first minute or so. Remove the open clams to the bowl.

11. Repeat covering and checking until all the clams have opened and been removed. If a clam refuses to open then throw it out. Do not force them open.

12. Add a bit more Sambuca (optional) and cook the liquid down for a few more minutes.

13. The pasta should be done. Turn the heat off from the clam pan, add the pasta.

14. Add a little of the pasta water and thoroughly combine.

15. Put the pasta in a bowl or plate, place the clams on top and add the chopped parsley to garnish.

Italians believe that cheese and seafood should not be combined. Mostly, that is because the salty parmesan would overpower the delicate seafood and over salt it. I happen to like a little on the pasta. Do what you like.

# Chapter 7
## PASTA

Pasta is perfect for one. Fresh pasta usually comes in amounts that are perfect for one, or at least you can buy just as much of it as you need. With dried pasta you can cook only as much as you need. It is inexpensive, lasts for a long time in the pantry and lasts for days in the refrigerator after it is cooked.

There are more recipes for pasta than any other single dish. The possibilities of creative and improvised pasta dishes are fun, easy and perfect for both people just learning to cook and expert chefs emptying the fridge. When I can't think of what to make, I make pasta.

One of the best aspects of pasta is that it is really inexpensive. Combined with a creative way to turn leftovers into tonight's meal, it really is a money saver. I don't think that I have ever looked in my fridge and not been able to come up with some sort of pasta dish. Even if all you have is a hunk of parmesan cheese, some olive oil and garlic you have the makings of one of the great Italian classics: "Aglio Olio".

Make sure that you keep plenty of different dried pastas in the cupboard. I have tried to explore a variety of different shapes and sizes here, but you should experiment and discover which shapes and sizes go best with what sauces and dressings. I love thick, wide noodles with meat-based sauce such as lamb ragu and I really enjoy seafood such as clams or shrimp with long, thin pasta.

You may be used to pasta dishes that are drenched in sauce. With a few exceptions, this is not how the Italians eat pasta. The sauce should just "dress" the pasta, coating the noodles, not drowning them. I recommend treating pasta just like salad: combine it in a pan or bowl then remove it to a serving plate or bowl, letting any excess sauce shake off as you serve it.

Pasta is a carbohydrate. It is a great source of quick energy and a wonderful and delicious way to put on a few pounds if you just sit around and do nothing. My wife often craves pasta leftovers for breakfast. This makes perfect sense. She has a very busy day ahead of her and her body tells her to fuel up.

Remember this when you fix yourself pasta. Carbohydrates are quick burning fuel, therefore eat it before you need this kind of energy and keep in mind your amounts when you are not going to be active after the meal. Above all, never drive yourself crazy and enjoy your meals. One night of a pasta fest and straight to bed will not turn you into Jabba the Hut.

# PENNE WITH FENNEL AND SAUSAGE

This recipe uses sausages, which are sometimes difficult to buy individually. The good news is that if you have to buy a package of 5 or 6 sausages, you won't have a problem eating them for the following breakfast, lunch or dinner. I often will eat a cooked sausage right out of the fridge as a snack. You can also freeze them.

I suggest that you buy locally made sausages, which tend to not have any junk in them. My local supermarket has both sweet and spicy turkey sausages. You can use whatever you like. Just remember (unless they are pre-cooked) always cook sausages thoroughly!

## INGREDIENTS
2 Sweet or Spicy Sausages
1 Fennel bulb
1 Pepper (orange, yellow or red)
2 Garlic cloves
2 Slices of Pancetta (diced)
Penne pasta
Olive oil
Heavy Cream (or half and half)
Parmesan cheese
Italian Parsley (optional)

## TOOLS
Slotted Spoon or Tongs
Chef's Knife
Chopping Board
Large Pan
Saute Pan
Grater

There are two choices for cooking the sausages; you can grill them (if your grill is quick, easy and easy to clean because, if not you will never cook them, right?) I usually just cook them in the same pan as I cook the rest of the dish.

1. Dice the pancetta.

2. Dice the garlic.

3. Chop the pepper.

4. Chop the fennel.

5. Heat a tablespoon of olive oil in a good size pan.

6. While this is heating, in a 4 or 5 quart pan fill it with enough water (about 5 cups) to cook a couple of handfuls of pasta and set the heat to boil.

7. In the sauce pan, over medium heat add the sausages (if you bought a pack of 5 or 6 you could cook them all now).

8. After they are brown on all sides add a splash of water and cook for another 5 to 10 minutes. Cooking sausages takes some getting used to because the length of time needed to cook changes depending on the size, the ingredients and the casing. Generally, it takes about twenty minutes to cook a package of sausages. The first few times cooking you may need to cut in the middle of one to make sure that it is not pink. Most sausages are made with either turkey or pork, both of which need to be cooked thoroughly.

9. Once they are thoroughly cooked, set them aside to cool.

10. Deglaze the pan with a little more olive oil and a splash of white wine. The idea is to get the stuck bits from the sausage unstuck and have a base of fat to cook the rest of the dish.

11. Add the pancetta to brown. Keep it moving so it doesn't stick or burn.

12. Turn the heat to medium and add the garlic.

13. Once the combined garlic and pancetta start to fill your nose with the most amazing smell in cooking, add the rest of the vegetables and stir occasionally.

14. Cut 2 sausages into bite size pieces (about 1/4"). Add those back to the pan and stir in.

15. The water should be boiling by now. Drop in a couple of handfuls of pasta.

16. The sauce should take about the same amount of time as the pasta. Dried pasta usually takes about ten to twelve minutes to cook to al dente.

17. Turn the heat off on the sauce and add a good splash of heavy cream. You can use half and half if you don't bother keeping heavy cream on hand.

18. Remove the pasta with a slotted spoon or tongs and add it to the sauce. Stir together.

Serve in a bowl with grated parmesan (please no green cans) and if you like, some chopped Italian, flat leafed parsley.

# RIGATONI WITH PROSCIUTTO AND ASPARAGUS

I first cooked this dish for myself when I was working in London. I was on my own one night and had a craving for this plate of pasta. This is a recipe that I have borrowed from my friend Kirk Francis. He is a fantastic person who happens to be a great cook, lover of music and production sound mixer. He wrote a cookbook that I hope by the time you are reading this you can also buy.

## INGREDIENTS
6-8 Asparagus sprigs
3-4 Slices of Prosciutto
Red Pepper Flakes
Clove Of Garlic
Handful of Rigatoni or Penne
Butter
Olive Oil
Parmesan
Italian Parsley (Optional)

## TOOLS
Slotted Spoon
Chef's Knife
Cutting Board
Large Pan
Sauté Pan
Small Sauté Pan (optional)
Grater

One of the best pieces of advice I ever got about preparing vegetables, especially asparagus (which tends to get dried out quite easily) is to soak it in ice water for about twenty minutes before you need to cook it. This restores some of the moisture, which seems to bring out the flavor.

1. Cut the hard end off the asparagus and soak in ice cold water.

2. Put a pot of well-salted water on to boil. This is the only chance you have to effectively season the pasta.

3. Quickly blanch the asparagus in the boiling water. My friend Kirk suggests that it is ready when the smell of asparagus is in the air. That is usually about 2 minutes or less.

4. Cut the tips off of the asparagus and slice the rest in about the same size pieces.

5. Cut the prosciutto into a nice size dice.

6. In a sauté pan, heat about a tablespoon of olive oil, adding the minced garlic and pinch of pepper flakes. Be careful not to burn the garlic.

7. Add the prosciutto and sauté until it starts to get crispy.

8. Add the asparagus (except the tips). Cook with the prosciutto until they are warm.

9. In a small sauté pan melt a pat of butter.

10. Cook the tips at fairly high heat for a couple of minutes. If you don't have an extra pan or don't feel like washing one later, you can do this in the middle of your main pan by scooting the ingredients off to the side, melting the butter in the middle and quickly sautéing the tips.

11. Add the cooked pasta to the asparagus/prosciutto mixture and turn off the flame. Stir to coat the pasta with the sauce.

Serve in a bowl with some good quality, grated Parmesan and the blanched tips on top. If you have some, roughly chop a small handful of Italian parsley and sprinkle over top.

# CHANTERELLE MUSHROOM PASTA

Q

This dish is best with fresh pasta, although the best that I've ever made happened to be with dried penne. The great thing about fresh pasta when you find it is that it usually comes in single, or at least small portions. This is a very quick dish to make and one of those that you pull out of your hat when you find fresh chanterelles at the market. They tend to be expensive, so keep an eye on the price and only buy them when they are reasonable or you are feeling flush. Remember though, you only need a handful, so the $20 per pound may only mean a few dollars to you. The Pancetta you can buy by the slice in most supermarket delis. There is a packaged one that almost all groceries carry, but the better quality and cheaper (because you only need a slice or two) is going to be at the deli counter.

## INGREDIENTS
1 handful of Chanterelle Mushrooms (dusted, not washed)
1 Piece of Pancetta (Diced)
1 Shallot (Diced)
Penne Pasta or Fresh Pasta of any sort
1/4 Cup Red Wine
1 Tablespoon Butter
2 Tablespoon Olive Oil
1 Tablespoon Heavy Cream
Chopped Italian Parsley
Parmesan or Pecorino

## TOOLS
Large pot
Sauté pan
Chef's Knife
Cutting board
Grater

1.  Fill your large pot half to ¾ full of water and put on high to boil.

2.  Sauté´ the Pancetta in olive oil in a pan. (The pancetta that I prefer is covered in pepper so I very rarely add any additional seasoning).

3.  Add the Shallots and sauté until translucent.

4.  Add a glug of whatever wine you are having. In the summer and early fall I recommend a provincial Rosé and in winter a Pinot noir.

5.  Reduce the wine by half.

6.  At this point, the water should be boiling. If you are cooking fresh pasta then this will only take a few minutes. If you are cooking dried then it will be more like 10 minutes.

7.  As the pasta is about done, add the chopped Chanterelle mushrooms to the sauce.

8.  Lower the heat to a simmer and continue to cook, stirring often.

9.  Add the pat of butter and cream. This amount of cream isn't enough to give this lactose intolerant writer any problems, so don't worry or, if you must, leave it out. If you don't have heavy cream you can use half and half.

10. Once the pasta is cooked, add it to the pan. Make sure not to add so much pasta that there isn't plenty of sauce for every bite. It's better to eat a little less and have more of this wonderful flavor per fork full.

11. Stir the pasta into the mixture and add a little more olive oil.

Serve in a hot bowl with freshly chopped parsley and grated parmesan or pecorino cheese.

# SAUTÉED SHRIMP AND ANGEL HAIR

The reason that you see this so often on Italian Restaurant menus is because it is cheap and quick to make and makes you feel like you are sitting in a trattoria on the Amalfi Coast.

**INGREDIENTS**
**6-10 Shrimp**
**1 Lemon**
**Zest from that Lemon**
**1 T Butter**
**Olive Oil**
**Red Pepper Flakes**
**2- 3 Cloves Garlic, minced**
**¼ Cup White Wine**
**Handful Angel Hair Pasta**
**Salt And Pepper**
**Italian Parsley, chopped**

**TOOLS**
**Large Pot**
**Sauté Pan**
**Chef's Knife**
**Cutting Board**

1. Clean the shrimp. If you have taken my advice from the Seafood chapter about shrimp, the cleaning should consist of a rinse and at the very most pinching off the tails.

2. Zest the lemon.

3.  Set the shrimp on a plate, drizzle with olive oil, a squeeze of lemon and light salt and pepper. Use good kosher or sea salt or even Fleur de Sel if you have some. The milder the salt the better.

4.  Put a large pot of water on to boil. Salt liberally.

5.  This is a good time to mince the garlic and chop the parsley. This dish takes so little time that all the prep can take place while the water is coming to a boil.

6.  Once the water is boiling add as much pasta as you would like to eat – a good handful.

7.  Heat a tablespoon of butter and a tablespoon of olive oil in a sauté pan.

8.  Add the minced garlic and red pepper flakes and gently sauté, being careful not to burn the garlic.

9.  Add the shrimp and sauté on both sides until the shrimp just turns white. This does not take more than a couple of minutes.

10. Add the wine and reduce by about half.

11. Turn the flame off and add the pasta to the sauté pan and mix together, coating the pasta with the mixture.

12. Toss in the lemon zest.

Serve in a bowl with the chopped parsley and a little drizzle of olive oil on top. Italians generally do not serve parmesan over any sort of seafood, but it is not law. Your choice, but I'll have some on mine.

 **BROCCOLI AND CHICKEN THIGH FARFALLA**

This is another classic Italian restaurant specialty, except most restaurants and recipes use the chicken breast. I think that (In the U.S.) chicken breasts – especially boneless, skinless chicken breasts – have no flavor. The darker meat of the thigh, in my opinion, is the only chicken part that you can buy separately that tastes good. Fortunately, they are usually inexpensive as well.

**INGREDIENTS**
2-3 Chicken Thighs (Off the Bone if available)
Handful of Broccoli, Cut or broken into Bite Size Pieces
Handful of Farfalla (Bow Tie) Pasta
½ Small Onion, Chopped
1 Clove of Garlic, Minced
¼ Cup Chicken Broth
¼ Cup White Wine
1 T Chopped Fresh Ginger
Olive Oil
Parmesan

**TOOLS**
Large Pot
Sauté Pan
Chefs Knife
Cutting Board
Poultry Cutting Board
Poultry Knife
Grater

1. Prep the broccoli, onion, garlic and ginger.

2. In the sauté pan, heat a few tablespoons of olive oil.

3. Sauté the onion and ginger.

4. Once the onion is translucent, add the garlic. This prevents the garlic from burning.

5. Put the water on to boil. Generously salt the water.

6. If you have boneless thighs then cut the chicken into chunks, salt and pepper and sauté with the onion mixture. If you had to buy thighs still on the bone it's not a problem. Sauté the chicken with the bone, remove from the pan when it's cooked, let it sit a few minutes and then pull the meat off the bone and cut it into bite size pieces.

7. Add the broccoli last and briefly sauté it.

8. If you had the bone in chicken, add back the pieces now.

9. Pour in the white wine and reduce by half.

10. Add the chicken broth and turn down the flame to simmer.

11. Cover the pan and let the sauce gently reduce.

12. Cook a generous handful of farfalla. When the pasta is done so should your sauce. Remove the cover, turn off the flame and toss in the pasta. Serve in a bowl with a generous amount of grated parmesan, salt and pepper.

## JENNIFER'S PUTTANESCA

Puttanesca is a very traditional Italian pasta, loosely translated as "Made by prostitutes". The clients of the Italian cat houses of yester year must have eaten well.

You will notice that this makes more than one serving. That is completely intentional. This is one of the many things that I love to eat again and again. You can freeze the leftovers if you like. I never bother as I like it the next day for lunch. My wife likes it the next day for breakfast.

### INGREDIENTS
1 14 oz Jar of Tomato Sauce
1/2 Cup Rough Chopped Kalamata Olives (pits removed)
2 Tins Anchovies, Chopped (packed in olive oil)
Fettuccini (fresh if possible)
1 Onion Chopped
3 Cloves Garlic, Minced
1 T Capers
3 T Olive Oil
1 Pat Butter
1/2 Cup Red Wine
1 Teaspoon Red Pepper Flakes
1 Teaspoon Dried Oregano
Salt And Pepper
Parmesan

### TOOLS
Large pot
Sauté pan
Chef's Knife
Cutting board
Grater

1. Gently heat the olive oil in the sauté pan

2. Add the onions and garlic and add in a pat of butter. Salt liberally to bring out the liquid from the onion.

3. Let these cook for quite some time, maybe 10 to 15 minutes over med-low heat, stirring occasionally. You want the onions to be completely translucent and start to caramelize. Do not burn them!

4. While the onions cook, chop the olives, anchovies and, if you decided to use whole tomatoes, chop them, too. Don't discard the oil in which the anchovies were packed. I know you are saying "yuk, anchovies". I am not asking you to eat them raw, or fillet them or even eat them on a pizza (which is delicious, by the way). I AM asking you to roughly chop them and add them to the sauce where they actually melt. In this dish, they just add a wonderful, salty flavor and tons of stuff that is really good for you.

5. Once the onions are ready, add two glugs of red wine (roughly 1/2 cup) and tomato sauce (or chopped tomatoes).

6. Let this come to a gentle boil so the alcohol cooks off. I usually don't cook with too much canned anything but the occasional simple tomato sauce, especially in the winter, makes things quick, easy and delicious. The other item in the can that I like is the Italian whole tomato from San Marzano. These have more flavor than any store bought fresh tomato and have become a staple in my pantry. If you are lucky enough to find San Marzano tomato sauce then use it.

7. Add the olives, capers, red pepper flakes, anchovies and the oil from the anchovies.

8. Let this simmer for as long as you have or a minimum of 20 minutes. Put the pasta water on to boil.

9. When the water is boiling, put the pasta in it and stir it around. Cook for as long as the package instructs. Fresh pasta is perfect for one because it usually comes in smaller batches than dried pasta. It also takes less time to cook. Usually between 3 – 5 minutes.

10. While the pasta cooks, add the oregano and salt and pepper to the sauce. Make sure you taste before adding salt as the anchovies will be very salty and you may not need any at all. Also remember that the cheese that you are about to add is also salty. Italians won't mind, they salt their salad.

Liberally coat a serving of pasta with the sauce and grate some parmesan over it.

## OLIVES

You can buy Kalamata olives with the pits already removed. The only hazard is that the machine that removes the pits does not always remove 100% of the pits. Alternately, pitting olives is easy. Cut them in half without cutting all the way through, then squeeze the pit out. You will get really quick at this with only a little practice.

# MAKING RISOTTO

I know risotto is not pasta. It is an Italian starch just like pasta and therefore takes up the same culinary space. You will see on most Italian restaurant menus the risotto dishes listed along side the pasta. In Italy, when risotto in served it replaces the pasta course.

Making risotto (like making pasta) is about cooking the starch and then adding the flavor. The flavor can be simple herbs or vegetables or already prepared protein such as chicken or shrimp. Once you learn to make one risotto you can make many. Because of this, I have only given you a few recipes. I have seen many variations over the years, but they are all essentially the same. Sometimes the onion or garlic is left out; sometimes the broth is vegetable or beef; sometimes the cheese is different or, in the case of seafood, left out.

In a few simple steps, here is how you make risotto:

1.  Cook onion and or garlic in oil until translucent

2.  Coat the rice with the fat, usually olive oil.

3.  Add broth a little at a time, stirring the rice each time until the rice puffs up and is semi soft.

4.  Add the flavor (shrimp, chicken, duck, veg. etc.)

5.  add the cheese (optional)

That is it. So some say it is hard to make, or it is really time consuming. There are the five steps. You be the judge. I think it is simple, hearty and delicious. I have never screwed it up yet.

# MEYER LEMON RISOTTO

Meyer lemons are a fantastic cross between a regular lemon and a sweet orange. They originated in China and were introduced to the United States by Frank Nicholas Meyer in California in 1908. For a long time quite rare, they are now available, when in

season, in better markets and California backyards. Whole foods and the like seem to carry them most of the time. If you can't find them use a regular lemon. Because the Meyer lemon tends to be milder and less acidic, it's a good idea to use a little less of a regular lemon. I don't normally make a big deal about specific ingredients, but this is one of my favorites. I love lemons, but they can easily overwhelm a dish and the Meyer does not. The next time you run across Meyer lemons remember this recipe.

## INGREDIENTS
1-2 Meyer Lemons
1/2 Cup Arborio Rice
2 Cups Chicken Broth
1/4 Diced White Onion
1 Clove Minced Garlic
1/4 Cup Grated Parmesan
1 Teaspoon Lemon Zest
1 Tablespoon Olive Oil
1 Tablespoon Finely Chopped Rosemary or Italian Parsley
Salt And Pepper
Sugar

**TOOLS**
**Chef's Knife**
**Paring Knife**
**Fine Grater**
**Medium Grater**
**Small Sauce Pan**
**Med Sauce Pan**
**Ladle**
**Wooden Spoon**

Zesting a meyer lemon does not produce as much zest as a regular lemon because of it's thinner skin. For this dish, that will be fine. The zest of one meyer lemon should be just right.

1. Zest one meyer lemon.

2. Once zested, peal the lemon, removing all the seeds, pith and any other tough white bits.

3. Roughly chop the remaining meat of the lemon.

4. In a little dish, sprinkle the lemon with a little sugar and set aside.

5. Chop the onion and garlic and grate the cheese. It's best to prep this all ahead of time, although I will often prepare the lemon and the cheese as the rice is cooking.

6. Pour the chicken broth in a small pan and add about 1/4 cup water and warm over low flame on the back burner. Some chicken broth comes in cans that are 2 cups or nearly 2 cups. Use one can and put a little more water in the pan if it is not quite 2 cups. I like to cut the broth with water as I find the broth on it's own overpowers the other flavors.

7. In another pan (in front of the broth pan) heat the olive oil.

8. Add the onion and garlic to the oil and sauté until the onion is translucent.

9. Slowly add the rice and stir until completely coated with the oil.

10. Add a couple of ladles of broth and stir.

11. Cook over med low heat. The concept of having to stir risotto constantly is nonsense. The reason for stirring is to expose all of the rice to the broth and more importantly keep it from sticking to the bottom of the pan. So, what I do is stir pretty thoroughly every time I put another ladle of broth into the rice.

12. Continue this process until all of the broth is absorbed and the rice has softened. This should take about 25-30 minutes.

13. Taste the rice. It should be al dente. If there is still any hardness give it another 5 minutes.

14. When it is done, turn the heat off and stir in the cheese and let it melt.

15. Add the lemon zest and sugared lemons. Stir together. If you like the taste of Rosemary add it now. I tend to leave it out in the summer. Instead, I prefer flat leaf Italian Parsley. It gives the risotto a fresh, spring or summer flavor any time of year.

16. Chop the parsley to somewhere between fine and rough. I like the occasional flake. Just try to keep the bigger stems out as they are tough and tend to be bitter.

17. Stir the parsley in and add a little pepper. Taste for seasoning but you should not need any salt. The cheese should provide enough salt on it's own.

## Use a Fine Grater to Zest Lemon

This dish is wonderful all on it's own. It also makes a great basis for grilled shrimp or chicken. My favorite is with an arrugula salad with Meyer lemon dressing. (See salads)

Risotto is hard work the first few times you make it. Once you get used to it you will want to make it all of the time. The variations are as many and varied as that other starchy product from Italy: pasta.

# ROASTED PUMPKIN RISOTTO

Roasting pumpkin for one serving of risotto does seem like a lot of trouble. The good news is that it is so delicious and easy to do that you can make it, eat it as your vegetable for another meal and put enough in a plastic container in the fridge to have in this risotto a few days later. Around Halloween is the perfect time. It's cold, pumpkins are obviously in season and you might feel like more than one pumpkin dish in a week.

## ROASTING PUMPKIN

Peel the pumpkin and cut in half. Clean out the inside seeds. (Roast them with a little sea salt for a great snack). Cut into bite sized cubes and place on a cookie sheet. Drizzle with olive oil and sprinkle with brown sugar (optional). Roast in a pre-heated 400º degree oven for about 45 minutes, until the pumpkin is easily poked with a fork.

Also consider roasting butternut squash or Brussels sprouts with the pumpkin.

## INGREDIENTS
1/2 Cup Arborio Rice
2 Cups Chicken Broth
1/4 Diced White Onion
½ Cup White Wine
½ Cup Roasted Sugar Pumpkin
1 Clove Minced Garlic
1/4 Cup Grated Parmesan
1 Tablespoon Olive Oil
1 Tablespoon Finely Chopped Sage
Salt And Pepper

## TOOLS
Chef's Knife
Paring knife
Grater
Small sauce pan
Med sauce pan
Ladle
Wooden spoon

1. Add ¼ cup of water to the broth and put it on medium heat.

2. In the larger pan heat a tablespoon of olive oil.

3. Add the onion and garlic. Sauté until the onion is translucent.

4. Stir in the rice until it is completely coated in oil.

5. Add the white wine and let the alcohol cook off.

6. Add a ladle full of broth and stir for a few minutes.

7. Continue to add the broth a little at a time, always being careful that the rice is always in a bit of liquid and is not sticking to the bottom of the pan.

8. Continue this process until the rice is puffy and nearly soft. This should take about 25-30 minutes.

9. Add the pumpkin and stir in. Cook for 5 minutes, stirring often.

10. Turn the heat off and stir in the cheese and sage.

11. Salt and pepper to taste.

One last note on the pumpkin: You can get either packaged or frozen pumpkin or butternut squash. Either or both will work for this recipe. If it has not yet been cooked, stick it on a cookie sheet with a little olive oil, brown sugar and salt and pepper. Stick it in the oven at 400 as you cook the rice. It should be soft by the time you are ready for it.

# ASPARAGUS RISOTTO

I made this for a vegetarian friend who absolutely loved it. If you are not a vegetarian, I would suggest the chicken broth instead of the vegetable broth.

## INGREDIENTS
1/2 Cup Arborio Rice
2 Cups Vegetable Broth (or Chicken Broth)
5-6 Stalks Asparagus
1/4 Diced White Onion
1 Clove Minced Garlic
1/4 Cup Grated Parmesan
1 Tablespoon Olive Oil
1 Tablespoon Finely Chopped Italian Parsley (Optional)
Salt And Pepper

## TOOLS
Chef's Knife
Fine Grater
Medium Grater
Small Sauce Pan
Med Sauce Pan
Small Frying Pan
Ladle
Wooden Spoon

1. Cut the hard end off of the asparagus and soak in a bowl of ice water for about 20 minutes.

2. Heat the broth in the small pan. If you are using chicken broth, I suggest that you add about a ¼ cup water to dilute it.

3. Sauté the garlic and onion in olive oil in the bottom of the medium pan.

4. Slowly add the rice, stirring it to coat with the onion mixture.

5. Add a ladle of broth and stir.

6. Continue this process for about 25-30 minutes.

7. In the sauté pan, sauté on pretty high heat the asparagus in butter. This should only take about 5 minutes.

8. When the rice is puffy and just beginning to be tender add the sautéed asparagus and stir in.

9. Cook for another 5 minutes.

10. Turn off heat and add the grated parmesan, stirring it thoroughly.

Serve with some Italian Parsley sprinkled on top.

# Chapter 8
## PIZZA

    My wife married me for my pizza. Long before we were together, she was attracted to me because I made a pizza that she loved. I'm not implying anything in particular; I'm just saying that it is not a bad idea to learn how to make pizza.

    Making great pizza is nearly as easy as calling one of those horrible, chain pizza delivery services. I recommend making your own instead. On the other hand, if you have a great local "mom and pop" pizza place at the end of your street like I do, then, by all means indulge from time to time.  It's quick and easy and usually cheap. Homemade pizza is different. It serves several purposes and can be just as convenient as Joe's at the end of the street, but will be much better, cheaper and just as quick and easy.

Pizza was invented to serve leftovers. So, anything in your fridge and pantry is a candidate for the top of your pizza. How do you think pineapple made it there? Sure, it requires some cheese and maybe a tomato sauce, but once you get used to whipping up a pizza for yourself you will regularly stock the essential ingredients. They store well and are really cheap.

So what about the dough? No, you are not going to buy frozen dough. NO! Step away from the freezer! Making dough is easy. I will give you two dough recipes here: one leaven (needs to rise) and one un-leaven. Both make great pizzas. But here is the key: both can be par baked (cooked for a minute or two) and FROZEN! Yes, that's right. Do not BUY frozen dough: make it. You can make dough once every couple of weeks and have 8-10 pizzas whenever you want. All you need to do is pop one out of the freezer, cover it with goodies and bake it for 8-10 minutes. So NOW does it seem like a big deal?

## PIZZA STONE

There is one essential piece of gear that you must have if you are going to make pizzas on a regular basis. A pizza stone is nothing more than a ceramic slab that sits in your oven and holds and conveys heat to the bottom of your pizza. You can buy a purpose built one for around thirty dollars. I used to also recommend unglazed tile as a substitute if you are really on a budget but my understanding is that there may be some health/safety issues with the material in the ceramic so it's not worth the risk.

I suggest the rectangular stones. The circular ones have less surface area and fit in fewer ovens. They may look like pizzas but they are far less practical. You can use an aluminium pizza pan or a cookie sheet but if you are serious about pizza, get a stone. They last for years.

# BASIC DOUGH

Making pizza dough is very similar to making bread. There really isn't much to the recipe or the process. Once you have done it and it works you will do it over and over without the least bit of thought. The guy down on the corner does it every morning before coffee.

## Ingredients
**4 Cups All Purpose Flour**
**1 ¾ Cup Warm Water**
**2 Tablespoons Olive Oil**
**1 Tablespoon Sugar**
**1 Teaspoon Active Dried Yeast**
**1 Teaspoon Salt**
**Corn Meal (for dusting)**

## Tools
**Stand Mixer, Food Processor or Large Mixing Bowl**
**Flat, Clean Surface such as marble to roll out dough**
**Rolling Pin**
**Chef's Knife or Pastry Knife**
**Pizza Peel (Wooden Paddle)**

You can do this in a bowl by hand, but the easiest way is with either a food processor or stand mixer.

1. In a measuring cup, combine the water the yeast, stir once and let sit for 5-10 minutes.

2. Once the yeast mixture starts to bubble, pour it into the mixing bowl and add the sugar and salt.

3.  Turn the mixer on low and add the flour and finally the olive oil.

4.  Beat on med. for about 10 -12 minutes. Use the hook if you have one.

5.  Cover with a clean kitchen towel and let sit to rise for an hour.

6.  Liberally flour a clean, flat, hard surface. (see sidebar).

7.  Divide the dough into as many baseball size balls as there is dough. With this amount of dough you should end up with between 8 and 10.

8.  Set them aside and cover with a towel.

9.  Take one of the balls and press it into a disc in the center of your rolling area.

10. Flour your rolling pin and start slowly rolling first in one direction then the other, turning and flipping the skin as you go. I think the only good pizza is a thin pizza, so roll it out thin. Don't worry about the shape. One of the charms of homemade pizza is the funny shape. If you are a real compulsive, you can use a plate and a sharp paring knife to create "perfect" round pies.

11. Place your pizza stone or whatever you are planning to cook pizza on in the oven and pre heat to 450º.

12. On a pizza peel (those big paddle things) sprinkle some corn meal. Corn meal works like ball bearings under the pizza.

13. Place one of your new, uncooked pizza skins on the peel and, with a quick flick of the wrist, place it on the pizza stone. Par Bake for about 2 minutes, remove and repeat for all of the skins that you are not planning on eating today.

Let the skins cool and place them in a large freezer bag. Stick them in the freezer and have a pizza whenever you want it. By the time you get all of the ingredients on it and the oven pre heated, it will be thawed and ready to cook.

## ROLLING SURFACE

In order to successfully roll out pizza, pie or any other dough, you need a surface that is flat, clean and hard.

You can probably use your countertop. When I had a tiled kitchen counter I used a roll out plastic sheet that very cleverly had pizza shapes printed on it. They were totally useless as they were immediately covered in flour, but the piece of plastic was a good idea. Anything will do as long as it is one solid piece (nowhere for the flour to hide) and can be cleaned up afterward.

Cooking stores sell big pieces of marble. They work great but are very heavy, hard to hold over the sink to clean and even harder to store. I know, I have one. It does work really well, though.

# UNLEAVENED PIZZA DOUGH

My favorite pizza is built on dough that is as much like a cracker as it is bread. Unleavened pizza dough is the ultimate in thin pizza. This recipe is as simple as it gets.

## INGREDIENTS
**2 Cups All Purpose Flour**
**1 Cup Semolina Flour**
**1 Cup Water**
**1 Teaspoon Salt**
**Corn Meal (for dusting)**

## TOOLS
**Large Mixing Bowl**
**Flat, clean surface such as marble to roll out dough**
**Rolling Pin**
**Chef's knife or pastry knife**
**Pizza Peel**
**Parchment Paper**

1. Combine the dry ingredients in a large bowl.

2. Slowly add in the water, stirring constantly. You can do this with a spoon or your hands.

3. On a clean, flat surface cover with flour and kneed the dough for about one minute.

4. Cut into 8-10 equal pieces and cover with a clean towel.

5. Press down one of the pieces to form a pancake.

6. Roll with well-floured rolling pin until paper-thin.

7. Repeat until all are flat. Stack on a plate using parchment paper to separate.

If you are not cooking 10 pizzas (which I often do for parties) freeze in a plastic freezer bag. They will defrost very quickly when you want a pizza.

## INVENT A PIZZA

Pizza was invented as a conveyance for leftovers. Creating your own pizza is as easy as opening your fridge. Pick a few ingredients, add some sauce and/or cheese and you too have invented a pizza.

# Q CLASSIC PEPPERONI PIZZA

My son insisted that this pizza be in the book. "How can you have pizza without the classic?" he asked. This is as semi-homemade as I get. All of these ingredients you can buy in a package or jar at your market. There is nothing fancy here but the end product is really great.

**INGREDIENTS**
**1 Pizza Skin (see above)**
**½ Cup Mozzarella Cheese**
**¼ Cup Tomato Sauce (In a jar with a lid)**
**Handful Sliced Pepperoni**
**Olive Oil**
**Corn Meal**
**Red Pepper Flakes**

**TOOLS**
**Pizza Peel (big, wooden paddle)**
**Pizza Cutter or Chef's Knife**
**Pizza Stone (see above)**

1. Place the Pizza stone in the oven and pre heat to 450º.

2. Dust the peel with corn meal and lay the skin out on it.

3. Evenly disperse the sauce. Spoon it on and use the back of the spoon to work a thin layer from the center out to the edge.

4. Arrange the pepperoni evenly in a single layer.

5. Cover with a thin layer of cheese.

6. Sprinkle with Red Pepper flakes.

7. Bake for 8-10 minutes, until the cheese is melted and the crust is a golden brown.

8. Remove from the oven using the peel and/or a large spatula.

9. Wait for 5 minutes to cool then cut into as many pieces as you would like.

That's right, you are supposed to put the pepperoni under the cheese. Don't knock it until you've tried it.

# Q PEAR AND PROSCIUTTO PIZZA

This is the one. My wife would probably still have married me because she is my soul mate, but it would have been much harder work on my part. This pizza is why she ever gave me the time of day in the first place.

Like most pizzas, this requires very little preparation. It is all about the ingredients. Buy some great prosciutto and some really good stinky cheese. This pizza sounds really simple but you will not believe how delicious it is.

## INGREDIENTS
**1 Pizza Skin (see above)**
**½ Small Hunk of Stinky Cheese (Camembert or whatever you like)**
**1 Ripe Pear, Thinly Sliced**
**4 Or 5 Thin Slices of Prosciutto**
**Handful of Fresh Arugula**
**Olive Oil**
**Corn Meal**

## TOOLS
**Pizza Peel**
**Pizza Cutter or Chef's Knife**
**Pizza Stone**

1. Place the Pizza stone in the oven and pre heat to 450º.

2. Dust the peel with corn meal. This keeps the pizza from sticking when you go to slide it into the oven.

3. Lay the skin out on the peel.

4. Evenly disperse the cheese. It will melt and spread out, so don't drive yourself crazy getting this too precise.

5. Evenly place the pear slices in a single layer.

6. Bake for 8-10 minutes, until the cheese is melted and the crust is a golden brown.

7. Remove from the oven using the peel.

8. Add the prosciutto in a single layer.

9. Top with a layer of arugula and drizzle with a little olive oil and some pepper (optional).

Always let pizza rest for a few minutes before cutting.

# ¢ MUSHROOM, POTATO AND GORGONZOLA PIZZA

Sometimes the most unlikely combinations make the greatest tastes. This is so true for this pizza. Force yourself to make it. This one takes a little more preparation than the other pizzas so plan for it. You will not be disappointed.

## INGREDIENTS
**1 Pizza Skin**
**1 Small Hunk Gorgonzola**
**2 or 3 Small White Potatoes**
**½ Small Onion**
**6-8 Mushrooms (Your Choice)**
**2 Tablespoons Finely Chopped, Fresh Rosemary**
**Olive Oil**
**Corn Meal**

## TOOLS
**Small Sauté pan**
**Pizza Peel**
**Pizza Cutter or Chef's Knife**
**Pizza Stone**

1. Place your pizza stone in the oven and pre heat to 450º.

2. Slice the potatoes into very thin coins.

3. Also slice the onion and mushrooms into thin pieces.

4. With a little olive oil, sauté the potatoes with some salt and pepper and about half of the rosemary.

5.  Sauté the potatoes for about 20 minutes over med. heat. Make sure that you cook the potatoes pretty thoroughly.

6.  Remove them to a bowl.

7.  Add a little more olive oil to the pan and add the onion.

8.  Salt onions and cook over low heat, stirring occasionally.

9.  When the onions become wilted and start to turn brown you can turn off the heat.

10. While cooking the onions, in a non-stick pan start to sauté the mushrooms. You should need very little, if any fat. I add a little salt to wick the moisture from the mushrooms. If anything, add a small pat of butter.

11. Sprinkle the corn meal on your pizza peel and place your skin on top of it.

12. Build the potato, onions and mushrooms on top of the pizza.

13. Evenly place little hunks of the cheese on top of the other ingredients.

14. Sprinkle the remaining rosemary over top of the pizza and get it in the oven. It should take about 10 minutes to be bubbly, nice and crisp.

You will think of sending me gifts when you eat this.

# FRESH TOMATO, BASIL AND MOZZARELLA

Q¢ This is a classic. Often referred to as a margherita since it was supposedly first made in Naples in honor of Queen Margherita, the reining monarch of Italy at the time. She must have been a woman of simple and exquisite taste, for this pizza is as good as any, with the right ingredients. Fresh Mozzarella is easy to come by these days but I only make this when I can get really sweet, ripe tomatoes.

## INGREDIENTS
**1 Pizza Skin (See Above)**
**1 Ripe Tomato, Thinly Sliced**
**1 Ball of Fresh Mozzarella, Thinly Sliced**
**6-8 Fresh Basil Leaves, Chopped**
**Olive Oil**
**Corn Meal**

## TOOLS
**Pizza Peel**
**Pizza Cutter or Chef's Knife**
**Pizza Stone**

1. Place the pizza stone on the center rack and Pre Heat the oven to 450º.

2. Slice the tomatoes, basil and mozzarella. You may have to search for good mozzarella. Fortunately, there are many good makers these days and most good grocers stock at least one of them. They are usually local, come packaged in water and are usually not terribly expensive.

3. Shake out a little corn meal onto the pizza peel and place the skin on top.

4. Drizzle with olive oil.

5. Cover the skin with a single layer of cheese,

6. then a single layer of tomatoes

7. followed by a sprinkling of basil. Save a little basil for after the pizza is cooked.

8. If you want to add a little spice you can sprinkle a few red pepper flakes at this point. I like to add just a dash more olive oil over the tomatoes.

9. Cook for about 10 minutes.

10. Remove from the oven using the pizza peel.

11. Let sit for a few minutes, then sprinkle with the rest of the fresh basil. This makes it taste fresh and lively.

Try a variation where you do not cook the tomatoes. Both ways are simple and delicious.

# Q¢ SAUSAGE PIZZA

This is not your Uncle Ernie's pizza. Go to the best grocery you have in your neighborhood and buy the best looking sausage. Many places sell them on their own, but if you have to buy a pack of sausages you can freeze the rest. You can also keep them in the fridge and have them later in the week.

## INGREDIENTS
**1 Pizza Skin**
**3 Tablespoons Grated Aged Gouda**
**1 Spicy Sausage (or mild if you like it that way)**
**1 Roasted Red or Yellow Pepper, Sliced**
**1 Tablespoon Finely Chopped Rosemary**
**Olive Oil**
**Corn Meal**

## TOOLS
**Pizza Peel**
**Pizza Cutter or Chef's Knife**
**Pizza Stone**
**Sauté Pan**

1. Place the pizza stone on the middle rack of the oven and Pre Heat to 450º.

2. Cut sausage out of casing and crumble into a sauté pan with a little olive oil.

3. Sauté until cooked. About 20 minutes.

4. Finely chop the rosemary.

5. Spread corn meal on a pizza peel.

6. Place skin on peel and liberally cover with the Gouda.

7. Once the sausage is cooked let it cool for a few minutes.

8. Layer the sausage over the cheese.

9. Arrange the peppers and sprinkle with the chopped rosemary.

10. Cook for 10 minutes, or until the cheese is all melted and the crust is golden brown.

11. Remove and let sit for a few minutes. Slice and serve.

There are many variations of this one. Mushrooms instead of sausage, goat cheese instead of gouda, different meat, different vegetable. Caramelized onions or leeks are amazing. Go nuts.

## ROAST A PEPPER

Take a fresh red or yellow pepper, drizzle it with a little olive oil and either place it on a gas burner, in a 400° oven or on the grill. Turn frequently until it is black on all sides. Let sit to cool then remove the skin. It should peel off quite easily. Cut off and discard the stem and seeds. Slice into slivers. Drizzle with a little more olive oil, salt and pepper.

# Q CELERY, PARMESAN AND TRUFFLE PIZZA

I know this one also sounds weird. The crunchy celery and the strong truffle make it really wonderful and different. If you have never had truffles before, be careful. First of all, they are very rare and even more expensive. You need to find them in the wintertime at a reputable cheese or gourmet shop. You will have to ask. They are usually not kept on the shelves. Truffle oil, on the other hand, is available year round and can be found at most grocers and gourmet shops. For this pizza, it is a reasonable substitute.

## INGREDIENTS
1 Pizza Skin
3 Tablespoons Grated Parmesan Cheese
2 Celery Stalks, Very Finely Chopped (On a Mandolin)
1 Tablespoon Shaved Black or White Truffle
or
 4-5 Drops Truffle Oil
Olive Oil
Corn Meal

## TOOLS
Pizza Peel
Pizza Cutter or Chefs Knife
Pizza Stone
Sauté Pan
Mandolin (optional)
Vegetable peeler (for shaving the truffle)

1. Pre-heat the oven to 450º.

2. Slice the celery very thinly. (with a mandolin if you have one)

3. Sprinkle corn meal on the pizza peel

4.  Place the skin on the peel.

5.  Drizzle with olive oil.

6.  Grate a layer of cheese.

7.  Arrange a single layer of celery.

8.  Drizzle with a little more olive oil.

9.  Bake for 10 minutes.

10. Grate a little more cheese on top and let sit for 5 minutes.

11. Shave several pieces of truffle on top or drizzle with truffle oil.

## PIZZA PARTY

Once you get the hang of making homemade pizzas, you might want to have a pizza party. Make a big salad, buy some olives and other snacks and make sure to have plenty of wine.

If you prepare all of the ingredients in advance and arrange them on your kitchen counter, everyone can pitch in and create variations. Get the party started with the potato pizza and a glass of wine. That should prime your guests to jump in and make their own.

## INGREDIENTS TO PREP IN ADVANCE

Roast and slice peppers
Sauté mushrooms of various types
Caramelize onions
Sauté potatoes
Sauté the sausage
Grate various cheeses
Slice tomatoes
Slice pepperoni
Chop vegetables
Chop herbs

When calculating how much food to have, I have found that if you figure roughly one pizza per person you will be covered. I would make sure that there are a few extra skins in the freezer just in case.

# Chapter 9
## COMFORT FOOD

    This topic will have lots of overlaps depending on your age and locale. I am originally from Ohio, but I lived in Boston for a long time. I then moved to California and was married to a high maintenance princess for an even longer time. Now I am married to a Kansas girl. Since I am on the road a lot, been divorced, lived in China, England and New York on my own, I have been not only cooking a lot for myself but I have often been in need of comfort food. I have also developed a rather broad range of what that might be. No longer do I strictly need mashed potatoes or spaghettiO's, although the former is still pretty near the top of the list.

One of my other gifts of cooking single meals comes to me as the default short order cook for our 5 children. This brings me to my first recipe in this chapter. My biological son had decided to become a 'pescatarian', (a vegetarian who also eats fish). He needed to be fed the other night. I had already had appetizers at a restaurant earlier and was not hungry. Pasta is always a safe bet with my son and the cupboard was full, but challenging. I suggested a rather complicated and experimental pasta dish when he asked: "Can we just have sauce, plain old?"

Most comfort food is based on people as much as places. I will never forget the smell of bacon in my grandmother's kitchen. She was a very petite, frail woman who had everything under the sun wrong with her. That did not stop her from cooking homemade corn bread and bacon nearly every day. She lived to be 90. Her green beans are in this chapter.

Different seasons also make me think of different comfort foods. When the tomatoes are ripe I love a bacon and really fresh tomato sandwich. I sometimes even skip the bacon, except it reminds me of my grandmother.

I hope you enjoy my comfort food and get inspired to try your hand at some of the dishes that remind you of your life, your family and your childhood.

# PENNE WITH SAUCE, PLAIN OLD

This is both the quintessential solo meal and comfort food, all made quickly and easily. What could be more comforting than a meal that can be made straight from the cupboard in a matter of minutes? I kid you not, this is dead simple. It always works and is perfect. Cooking does not have to be complicated to be good. If that were not true, Italy would not exist.

## INGREDIENTS
**Handful of Penne**
**Can of Tomato Sauce**
**Red Pepper Flakes**
**Dried Thyme**
**3 Cloves of Garlic, Minced**
**Sea Salt and Pepper**
**Grated Parmesan**

## TOOLS
**Large Pan**
**Sauce Pan**
**Chopping Board**
**Medium Grater**
**Chef's Knife**
**Wooden Spoon**

1. Boil some water. I always use a pasta double boiler but a regular pan of water will do for a single serving of pasta.

2. Salt the water liberally with sea salt.

3. I have said this before but dried pasta does not easily go bad. You can use a handful out of a box and use the rest another day. Alternately, you can cook the whole package and save the leftovers in a plastic bag in the fridge. You never know if you might want more or someone might drop by. You may be so impressed with this quick meal that you take your neighbor a bowl full!

4. In a saucepan, heat the sauce, garlic, thyme, pepper flakes and salt and pepper.

5. Cook it for the length of time that it takes to boil the water and cook the pasta.

Serve the pasta in a bowl mixed with as much sauce as your comfort level requires. Grate some fresh parmesan over the top. If you don't really need that much comfort and would just like a delicious pasta, add some fresh, chopped Italian parsley as well.

# PASTA WITH BUTTER AND A SIMPLE SAUCE

Jeopardy occasionally has the "Stupid Answer" category where all of the answers are like: "The body buried in Grant's Tomb". Writing this down is a little like that. The reason that I have included this is to remind you to have this every now and then. Budgets are tight, we all forget or don't want to go to the store and want something easy, comforting and cheap (to eat!!!). When I was in college, Sundays were the perfect time for this dish. The money had usually run out, the stores were closed and the Sunday Blahs had set in.

## INGREDIENTS
**Handful of Penne or Fettuccini**
**Tablespoon of butter**
**Grated parmesan**

**Butter Leaf Lettuce**
**Olive Oil**
**Aged Balsamic Vinegar**
**Salt and Pepper**

## TOOLS
**Large Pan**
**Medium Grater**
**Mixing Bowl**
**Wooden Spoon**

1. Boil Water.

2. Cook a handful of pasta.

3. Drain the water and add a good couple of pats of butter and a tablespoon or so of olive oil to the pasta. Stir together and let the butter melt.

4. Grate some parmesan, toss and put in a bowl or plate.

5. Pepper to taste. Skip the salt as the cheese usually fulfils this need.

6. Wash a handful of butter leaf lettuce or any of your favorite lettuce leaves (remember the darker in color, the better for you). I like butter lettuce for this meal because it stays with the theme.

7. Toss in a big bowl with a tablespoon of olive oil, a few drops of balsamic vinegar and salt and pepper. Toss this with your (clean) hands and make sure the leaves are well coated.

8. Place on a plate, leaving any excess dressing in the bowl.

Most Italians eat the salad after the main course. Italians make great movies, great cars and great lovers. Why not try it!

# SMASHED POTATOES

Where I come from, mashed potatoes are number one on the list of comfort foods, usually accompanying a steak or chicken. For tonight, I suggest that you pick up something at the store deli. I don't really condone fast food unless it is simple, healthy, has no crap in it and is as cheap as you can make it at home. My local deli makes a tasty roasted chicken.

## INGREDIENTS
**Half Dozen Red or White Potatoes, Quartered**
**1/4 Cup Buttermilk**
**2 Tablespoons Butter**
**Pinch Cayenne Pepper**
**Salt And Pepper**

## TOOLS
**Large Pan**
**Chef's Knife**
**Cutting Board**
**Potato Masher or Fork**

1. Boil the potatoes in enough water to completely cover them. They are done when a fork easily penetrates them. (20 min)

2. Pour off the water; add the buttermilk, butter and cayenne.

3. Smash up with a potato masher (or fork for a workout).

4. Salt and pepper to taste.

You can use some electric device if you want, but I prefer a simple, hand held masher. You don't have to plug it in and it is really easy to clean (as long as you clean it right away!).

# CHICKEN AND RICE

I didn't grow up with this dish but I have come to accept it as an old favorite. It is nearly impossible to screw up and you can even make it if you don't feel all that well, since it has nothing in it that is not soothing. The perfect cure for the common cold.

**INGREDIENTS**
**1 Boneless/Skinless Chicken Breast**
**Or**
**2 or 3 Thighs**
**4 oz Button Mushrooms**
**1 Cup Long Grain Rice**
**2 Cups Chicken Broth**
**1/2 White Onion, Chopped**
**2 Cloves Garlic, Minced**
**2 Tablespoons Olive Oil**
**Salt and Pepper**

**TOOLS**
**Sauté Pan**
**Chef's Knife**
**Cutting Board**

1. Wash and season the chicken.

2. Sauté the garlic and onion in the olive oil.

3. Add the chicken and the mushrooms.

4. Sauté the chicken so it is cooked on the outside (about 10 minutes, flipping after 5).

5. Add the rice and broth. Turn the heat up to bring the liquid to a boil.

6. Turn down to simmer and cover.

7. Cook for 20 minutes, or until all of the liquid has evaporated. You may need to take the top off for the last few minutes.

Serve with a glass of juice or water (or whiskey if you are really ill).

Chase with Nyquil and go to bed.

## UNTIDY JOSEPHS (AKA SLOPPY JOES)

Where I come from, you can get a Sloppy Joe in just about every greasy spoon. My mother made the only ones that I truly loved. Maybe that's why I have chosen to include this recipe in the Comfort Food section.

The nickname comes from my brother who always had a (different) way with words. I have done my best to make this as close to my mother's as possible, but I am afraid one important ingredient is not available in my area: Brooks Catsup. Not just because of the namesake, but because it was a bit spicy and a sort of spice that is not easy to replicate, especially considering all the years that have past since I last tasted it.

## INGREDIENTS
½ Pound Ground Beef
2 Tablespoons Yellow Mustard
4 Tablespoons Catsup
½ Small Chopped Onion
2 Cloves Minced Garlic
1-2 Tablespoon Sweet Pickle Relish
(If you really like it use 2)
1 Teaspoon Brown Sugar
Salt And Pepper
1 Tablespoon Worcestershire Sauce
A Few Drops of Tabasco Sauce or
A Pinch of Cayenne Pepper
Olive Oil
Onion or Plain Hamburger Buns

## TOOLS
Sauté Pan
Chef's knife
Chopping Board

1. Gently sauté the onion and garlic in just enough olive oil to keep it from sticking. Sauté until the onion is translucent, about 5-10 minutes.

2. Add the beef and let it brown.

3. Add plenty of Salt and Pepper as the meat browns.

4. Stir in the rest of the ingredients, cover and let simmer for about 20-30 minutes. The flavors need to congeal. When I make this for my family I never get a chance to let it simmer that long as they always insist on eating it.

Serve on a hamburger bun with some Conn's Potato Chips. If you are not within the distribution radius of Zanesville, Ohio for the Conn Potato Chip Company, then you will just have to improvise with some inferior, fried chip. I like a little piece of sharp cheddar cheese melted over my Joseph. Also, I think the really plain, small, white, cheap enriched buns are the best. They are nothing more than a porous vehicle for the Joe.  I hope this gives you as much pleasure as it does me.

## GROUND BEEF

You won't find much ground beef in my diet. But when I do eat it this is how I buy it: I go to the grocery or butcher and pick out something that is on sale. Often I buy tri-tip roast. I never, ever buy ground meat in a package. Take the piece of meat that you have selected (preferably boneless) and ask the butcher to double grind it. This way you have seen the piece of meat that you are eating and fortunately, 99% of butchers are happy to help.

# BACON AND TOMATO SANDWICH

This is a breakfast staple in the summer. My wife peals the tomatoes when she makes it but I rarely bother. This is a little like writing down sliced tomatoes as I assume most of you could figure out how to make a BLT. So consider this a reminder, if nothing else.

## INGREDIENTS
**3 Strips of Really Good Bacon**
**Lettuce or Arugula (optional)**
**1 Beautiful, Ripe Tomato, sliced and marinated in Olive Oil, Salt and Pepper**
**Sourdough Bread, lightly toasted (or something of your choice)**
**Mayo (optional)**

## TOOLS
**Chef's Knife**
**Cutting Board**
**Toaster (Optional)**

A word on bacon: There was the great bacon scare of the 1980's when people thought that a piece or two of cured, fried pig was a bad thing. HOGWASH! Don't eat bacon if you don't want to, but my grandmother ate bacon every day of her life and she died in her sleep at age 90. Her house constantly smelled of bacon grease and cornbread (which was cooked in bacon grease). But, I am certain that the bacon that she ate was simple and did not contain nitrates or any other unnatural curing agents. Salt is all that is necessary to cure bacon. So, go out of your way to find bacon that is naturally cured and has no anything in it other than bacon. It's out there. If your market doesn't carry it you can request it and they can and usually will get it.

# MAC AND CHEESE

My son ate nothing but frozen mac and cheese for years. It was actually pretty good. I did not grow up eating such a thing, so it wasn't until I had the current Mrs. Brooks' "homemade" Mac and Cheese that I begin to appreciate it's lusty comfort. Since we have five kids between us, Jennifer tends to cook for an army. I spent a lot of time making this recipe work for one, but feel free to add or subtract anything. It's hard to go wrong with all of this decadence.

## INGREDIENTS
1 Cup Elbow Macaroni
1 Cup Milk
½ Cup Shredded Cheddar Cheese
1/3 Can Cream of Mushroom Soup
½ Small Onion, chopped
1 Teaspoon Dried Mustard
1 Teaspoon Paprika
2 Tablespoons Sour Cream
½ Stick Butter
½ cup Bread Crumbs
Salt and Pepper

## TOOLS
Med Sauce Pan
Small Baking dish (an individual loaf pan or the smallest Pyrex pan will work)
Chef's Knife
Chopping Board

1. Pre Heat the oven to 350º.

2. Fill the saucepan a little more than half way with water and set on high heat to boil.

3.  Salt the water.

4.  When boiling, add macaroni.

5.  Cook until al dente (about 10 minutes).

6.  Butter the bottom and sides of the baking dish.

7.  Pour off the water, leaving the macaroni in the pan.

8.  Turn off the heat.

9.  Add half of the butter, half of the milk and all of the other ingredients (except the bread crumbs) and stir together in the pan.

10. Pour the mixture into the buttered dish.

11. Add the rest of the milk.

12. Shake the bread crumbs evenly over the mixture and add pats of the remaining butter.

Bake for 40 minutes. Serve with a blanket and cartoons.

## NEW YORK TIMES SAUSAGES AND MABEL'S GREEN BEANS

Since I began writing this book, one of my main concerns was the price of cooking for one. There is no doubt that cooking for one is more expensive per person than cooking for two, if not exactly double in many cases. And, since I encourage making enough for two just in case, it really is the same.

Because of my acute awareness of the prices, I am always on the lookout for great meals that don't end up having zeros in them. I figure if you can actually go to the grocery to buy the ingredients for the evening meal (not cereal, toilet paper and a 12 pack of Bud) and spend under ten dollars you have done good. Yes, I know you can go to McDonalds for under ten dollars. Bookmark your place here and go rent "Supersize Me". Trust me, you'll be back.

This brings me to sausages. I love sausages. You have to be careful where you buy them, but usually your local butcher or supermarket has freshly made sausages of all sorts. I like pork or lamb, but the turkey sausages at my local Gelson's are some of the best sausages I have ever had. Sausages freeze really well so you can always have them on hand. They are perfect summer food. You can stick them on the grill without any preparation whatsoever, turn them every now and then and that's it.

So this recipe is for the side dish. I have to give credit to the New York Times for the idea of putting the sausages together with green beans, but this recipe I have been eating since I was a baby and I mean literally a baby. My mother used to mash this up and feed it to me before I had teeth.

# MABEL'S GREEN BEANS

You are looking at the amount of ingredients at this point and saying to yourself, "this is not a dish for one!" (I presume you talk to yourself. I know I certainly do… or to the dog.) The truth is that this is not a dish for one. Well, not technically. I always cook this for myself with the intention of having leftovers.

## INGREDIENTS
**1/2 Pound Fresh, Crisp Green Beans**
**2 Medium Potatoes**
**1 White or Yellow Onion**
**2 Cups Chicken Broth**
**2 Slices of Bacon (optional)**
**Salt and Pepper**

## TOOLS
**4-6 Quart Pan**
**Cutting Board**
**Chef's Knife**

1. Rinse the beans under cold water, trim the ends and either cut or snap into one-inch pieces.

2. Cut the potatoes into nice, bite size chunks.

3. Same with the onion.

4. In a large saucepan cook the bacon for a few minutes. In this case, it is not necessary for the bacon to get crispy, just let off some fat. I say that the bacon is optional because some don't like it. It was not optional in my family. I did make this the other day knowing that I was serving it to someone who didn't eat bacon and it was nearly as good.

5. Once the bacon has cooked, deglaze the bottom of the pan with a bit of olive oil.

6. Add the green beans, potatoes, onions and the broth.

7. Salt and Pepper.

8. Add a couple of cups of water to cover everything.

9. Bring to a boil and then simmer forever. At least one hour, so the potatoes are really soft and a lot of the liquid has evaporated.

Grill yourself a couple of sausages and enjoy the beans. They will keep (and get better) for three or four days. I don't know after that, they never last that long in my house.

# Chapter 10
## SUNDAYS

When the weekend comes in my world the phones and email stop and I decompress. I often still work, but I make time for activities that I normally don't have enough time for during the week. Many of these activities take place in the kitchen.

There is time for bread to rise and cookies to bake. Sundays are perfect for simmering. That means that a pot of soup or some other dish that is slow but not too taxing and that will last well into the week will be on my stove.

My morning is usually when all of the kitchen activity begins. I don't get to bothered by leaving dirty dishes in the sink on Saturday night so Sunday morning starts by cleaning up that mess. Since I'm already in the kitchen, I begin thinking about what I am cooking for the day and the week. By the time I finish the dishes from the night before I have begun dirtying the next batch.

I don't spend the entire day in the kitchen, but I don't mind coming and going and making it my base for the day. I casually come and go. I don't like to cook things that have to be timed out to closely. This is the kind of cooking that I find relaxing: A little chopping, a glass of wine or iced tea, read a few chapters of my book, some more chopping, a nap, some simmering...

In this chapter are some of my favorite Sunday dishes. Most are about the time needed, but some are just about the feeling of rest and relaxation that mark most Sundays. And, of course the need for comfort from the Sunday blahs that will inevitably invade one's world as night falls.

Banana Nut Bread cooling on the windowsill.

# CHICKEN POT PIE

This recipe could go in many chapters in this book. I've chosen it to be a Sunday recipe because it takes a little time, it makes enough to have for leftovers the next day and even the next and it warms a cold winter Sunday at home.

It is a pie so we will use a traditional, flaky piecrust recipe. The filling for this pie has many options. If you have a left over part of a roasted chicken or turkey then use it instead of buying and cooking chicken. You can use whichever vegetables you have on hand and/or like. This recipe is with all fresh vegetables but you can easily substitute the carrots, peas and corn for 2 cups of frozen vegetables, especially in the winter.

## INGREDIENTS
**3 Cups All Purpose Flour + 3 Tablespoon Flour**
**4 Teaspoons Sugar**
**1 Teaspoon Salt**
**¾ cup Butter (chilled)**
**½ Cup Crisco (chilled)**
**1/2+ Cup Ice Water**
**1 Egg**

**1 ½ Lbs Boneless, Skinless Chicken Breast (or Breast and Thigh)**
**1 Chopped Onion**
**2 Chopped Celery Stalks**
**1 Cup Mushrooms (your choice)**
**2 Chopped Carrots**
**½ Cup Peas**
**½ Cup Corn**

**TOOLS**
**Large Mixing Bowl**
**Large Sauté pan**
**Cutting board**
**Chef's knife**
**Ceramic Pie Plate (or aluminium disposable)**
**Fine Sifter or Strainer**
**Pastry Dough Blender (optional)**
**Cookie Sheet**

1. Sift 3 cups of flour, the sugar and salt together in a large mixing bowl.

2. Cut in the butter and Crisco a little at a time using the dough blender or a couple of knives. I know, you haven't heard of using Crisco for a long time. Don't panic, it's only vegetable shortening and it is what makes the crust flaky.

3. After mixing gently, slowly drip in the water as you work the fat into the flour. You may need slightly more or less water. You want the dough to be the consistency of oatmeal.

4. Once you have that, form two equal discs, wrap them in plastic wrap and refrigerate for at least ½ hour. This is a good time to go read the newspaper or take a nap.

5. Pre-Heat the oven to 400º.

6. Cut the chicken into bite sized chunks.

7. Sauté the onion, carrots, mushroom, celery and any other fresh vegetables.

8. When you are finished, remove them to a bowl.

9. Add a little butter and olive oil to the pan then add the chicken.

10. Salt and Pepper generously as you briefly cook the chicken. Just cook it until it is barely white on all sides. If you are using yesterday's roasted chicken, just sauté briefly to impart the other flavors to it.

11. Remove with a slotted spoon into a separate mixing bowl.

12. Add the vegetables to the chicken, also using the slotted spoon. You should end up with around 5 cups of vegetables all together. You don't want any excess liquid from either the chicken or veg.

13. Add 3 tablespoons flour or wondra to the pan. If there is not enough liquid to dissolve it use a little water or chicken broth. Not much. You want a thick, light gravy.

14. Cook for a couple of minutes, scraping off any excess chicken bits from the pan.

15. Add that gravy to the chicken and vegetable mix. You can substitute a can of cream of mushroom or cream of broccoli soup if you are so inclined.

16. Roll out your dough into two round (ish) flat pieces that are big enough to more than cover the pie dish.

17. Carefully place one piece over the dish and tuck it in, cutting the excess off, but leaving an even amount (1/2 inch) hanging over.

18. Fill the pie shell with your filling all the way to the top.

19. Cover with the other dough piece.

20. Trim it a little past the edge so there is enough to crimp the two pieces together.

21. With a sharp knife cut several slits near the center. This will allow some of the steam to release as it bakes.

22. In a small bowl, combine the egg and about ¼ cup of water with a fork.

23. Lightly brush the top of the pie with the "egg wash". This will protect your flaky crust and help it become a beautiful golden brown. I have forgotten this step without a huge difference in result but it does work. Don't feel bad if you don't have an egg, a brush, a small bowl or don't feel like doing this. You will still have a delicious pie.

24. Place the pie on a cookie sheet in the oven and bake for 50 – 60 minutes at 400º. The pie should be golden brown on the top.

Let it sit for at least another 10 minutes before serving.

# POTATO AND LEEK SOUP

As described before about soup, it's never just for one meal. This is hearty and as good or better the next day. I suggest some rustic bread or a grilled cheese to be served with it.

## INGREDIENTS
4 Medium Potatoes (Red or White)
4 Leeks
2 Celery Stalks
3 Cloves Garlic
1 Tablespoon Olive Oil
6 Cups Water or Broth
3 Slices of Bacon
Fresh Thyme
Fresh Rosemary
1 Bay Leaf
Splash of Cream

## TOOLS
4-6 Quart Pan
Cutting Board
Chef's Knife

1.  Cook the bacon over medium heat in the bottom of the pan until it is crispy.

2.  Remove and set aside on a paper towel covered plate.

3.  Add some olive oil to the bacon grease and sauté the sliced garlic.

4.  Deglaze the pan with either a glug of white wine or beer.

5. Cut the stalk and tip off the leeks and slice them in half, lengthwise.

6. Rinse under cold water, fanning out to get rid of any sand and grit.

7. Slice into half coins.

8. Add the leeks and chopped celery to the pan with a bit more olive oil.

9. Salt and pepper.

10. Cook leeks and celery until they are soft.

11. I grate a little nutmeg at this point, although this is strictly optional and may be more of a subtle secret ingredient than a key taste.

12. Add potatoes and cover with chicken broth and/or water.

13. Add whole sprigs of herbs and more salt and pepper.

14. Bring to boil then reduce to simmer and cover for about an hour.

15. Turn the heat off, remove the sprigs and stir in cream. I often use half and half as this is really mostly about texture. You could even just use milk. You don't need much. Leave it out if you don't like or can't tolerate milk products.

This is one of the occasions that I use the one electric indulgence in my kitchen. I blend with a stick blender (sometimes called an emersion blender). It makes the soup creamy smooth and velvety. This is strictly optional and I don't always do it. I sometimes like the rustic chunks of potato instead.

You can also put the hot soup in a blender. Be careful when you do this. Do not fill the blender all the way to the top, blending a little bit at a time and make sure to cover the lid with a dish towel as an additional precaution and hold securely.

## How to Clean and Cut Leeks

Trim the stem and leaf ends off.

Cut lengthwise down the middle.

Rinse by fanning out under water.

Cut into half coins.

# STOLEN SOUP

The French Laundry was the most wonderful restaurant in the world. Sally and Don Schmidt owned and operated this beautiful little brick building in Yountville, Ca. in the heart of Napa wine country. It was an incredibly casual place that served the most sublime food I have ever tasted. Once you sat down and got a glass of wine you could wonder outside in the summer, or down into the kitchen to see how the main course was coming. Because there were only a dozen or so tables and Sally only prepared one main course per night along with several starters, desserts and surprises, she was always relaxed and not inundated with the usual chef's chaos.

One of the meals that I was privileged enough to enjoy at the French Laundry inspired this soup. It was not the same, but it was so unique and amazing that I was still thinking about it months later and came up with this recipe. So, if you are ever in the Anderson Valley, stop by Schmidt's Organic Apple Farm and thank Sally for the inspiration and buy some delicious organic apple butter.

## INGREDIENTS
**32 oz Low Sodium Chicken Broth**
**6 Tomatillos, Peeled and Sliced**
**2 Large Leaves of Sorrel (or Cilantro) Chiffonade (See P. 46)**
**2 Roma Tomatoes, Quartered**
**2 Oranges, Peeled and Chopped**
**2 Sprigs of Thyme, Stemmed and Finely Chopped**
**Sea Salt and Fresh Ground Pepper**

## TOOLS
**Large Pan**
**Chopping Board**
**Chef's Knife**

1. Heat the broth with the sliced tomatillos.

2. Add half the thyme and sorrel.

3. Salt and pepper.

4. Simmer for an hour.

5. Add the tomatoes and oranges along with the rest of the thyme and taste for final salt and pepper.

6. Simmer for another ten minutes and serve.

If you want to have some of this soup for leftovers, before the last step pour half of the soup into another pan. Only chop half of the tomato and orange, saving the rest for the next day. You want the tomato and orange to be fresh and still lively, not soggy.

# POTATO AND YELLOW PEPPER SOUP

This hearty, sweet soup is great year round. It is warming and delicious in the winter and great served chilled in the summer. Potatoes and peppers are always available.

Different color peppers can also be used. Try spitting the recipe in two or doubling it with two different colored peppers cooked separately and then go nuts with the presentation.

## INGREDIENTS
4 Golden Potatoes, Cubed
1 Yellow Onion, Chopped
6 Cloves Garlic, Minced
2 Yellow Peppers, Cubed
1 Jalapeno Pepper, Finely Chopped
1 14oz Can Chicken Broth
3 Cups Water
1 Tablespoon Extra Virgin Olive Oil
1 Tablespoon Fresh Thyme
Sea Salt And Fresh Ground Pepper

## TOOLS
Large Pan
Chopping Board
Chef's Knife

1. Heat the oil, garlic and onion in the bottom of a 5 or 6 quart heavy sauce pan.

2. Cook over med heat until onions are translucent.

3. Add broth, water, potatoes, salt and pepper.

4. Cover and cook over high heat for 20 minutes.

5. Add thyme, yellow pepper and more salt and pepper and reduce heat.

6. Cook for another 15 minutes.

7. Add more salt and pepper along with the jalapeno and simmer for another 5 minutes.

I suggest that you then blend until smooth with a stick blender or regular blender. Serve with a fresh sprig of thyme or Italian parsley sprinkled on top. For a variation, you could float a piece of baguette (toasted) along with a few slivers of grilled yellow or orange or red pepper. Also you can add a touch of cream.

# ROASTED PUMPKIN SOUP

There is something about cooking pumpkin that I love. I think it has to do with being frightened when I was little by those nasty looking things on people's porches around Halloween. I think I like the idea of getting back at them by eating them.

## INGREDIENTS
1 Small Sugar Pumpkin
3 Roma Tomatoes
1 Butternut Squash
2-3 Cups Chicken Broth
4 Slices Pancetta (Most
 of the fat removed), Diced
Splash Of Cream
Pomegranate Seeds
3 Shallots
1 Tablespoon Sage (Fresh if possible)
1 Pinch Cinnamon
Olive Oil
Splash of White Wine

## TOOLS
Non-Stick Cookie Sheet
Large Pan
Chopping Board
Chef's Knife
Blender

1. Peel and clean the pumpkin and squash and cut into roughly 1" chunks.

2. Arrange on a non-stick cookie sheet; drizzle with olive oil, salt and pepper.

3. Roast in the oven at 350º for 45-50 minutes or until soft. You should be able to easily poke a few of them with a fork.

4. Remove and let cool.

5. Par-boil the tomatoes in a pan of boiling water to remove the skin. It usually takes about 2 minutes in the water. They are ready to peel when the skins start to crack.

6. In the bottom of a soup pan, sauté the diced pancetta in a little of the olive oil until it is crispy.

7. Set aside on a paper towel covered plate to absorb excess grease.

8. Deglaze the pan with a little more olive oil and a glug of wine.

9. On low heat, sauté the shallots in that reduced liquid.

10. When they are translucent, add tomatoes, squash, pumpkin and enough broth to cover.

11. Briefly bring to a boil, then cover and simmer for 20-30 minutes.

12. This is a good time to remove the pomegranate seeds.

13. Add cinnamon and chopped sage and simmer for another 10 minutes.

14. Blend to a velvety consistency. Add cream and stir.

Serve in a hot bowl with a sprinkling of the crispy pancetta and a handful of pomegranate seeds.

# REALLY GOOD SOUP

One great way to create and discover new soups is by cooking whatever you find in the fridge. This is an example that works so well that I have repeated it many times. The carrots, celery and onion are the classic trio known by French chefs as mirepoix.

## INGREDIENTS
3 Carrots, Chopped
3 Stalks Celery, Chopped
1 Onion, Roughly Chopped
3 Garlic Cloves, Minced
2 Cans of Chicken Broth
4 Pieces of Thinly Sliced Prosciutto, Cubed
1/3 Cup White Wine
1 Teaspoon Red Pepper Flakes
2 Tablespoons Olive Oil
1 Pat Butter
2 Red Gala Apples
Sprigs of Rosemary And Thyme

## TOOLS
Large Pan
Chopping Board
Chef's Knife
Blender

1. In the bottom of a large soup pan first sauté the prosciutto in the olive oil and butter, then shortly thereafter add the garlic and onion.

2. Lightly salt the onion to bring out it's liquid. Not too much though as the prosciutto is already salty.

3. Add the carrots and celery and sauté for a few more minutes.

4. Add the white wine and turn the heat up to reduce the wine.

5. When it is reduced by half add the apple and broth.

6. Sprinkle the red pepper flakes and some pepper.

7. Bring to a gentle boil then reduce heat to a simmer.

8. Add the sprigs of rosemary and thyme. Cover and let simmer for about an hour.

9. Remove the herbs and blend with a stick blender.

What goes better with soup than a nice, homemade bread.

## ROSEMARY CIABATTA

There is nothing that goes better with a Sunday soup than a loaf of homemade bread. You can and should learn to make a loaf of bread. It sounds daunting, but think about it for a second: bread, in one form or another, is a staple food all over the world. Everyone is baking bread every day. How hard could it be? Once you do it you will feel like you have conquered your kitchen. It will take a bit of time, so that is why it's a Sunday activity.

I love Italian bread and I love it for the same reason that I love the rest of Italian cooking: it's simple, relies on good, fresh ingredients and is always delicious.

## INGREDIENTS
4 ½ Cups Flour
2 ½ Cups Warm Water
2 Teaspoons Active Dried Yeast
1 Teaspoon Sugar
1 Teaspoon Fine Sea Salt
1 Tablespoon Finely Chopped Rosemary
1 Tablespoon Olive Oil
Corn Starch

## TOOLS
Heavy Duty Electric Stand Mixer with Bread Hook or
Heavy Duty Electric Hand Mixer with Paddle
Pizza Stone or Cookie Sheet
Pizza Peel (Optional)
Rubber Spatula
Wire Rack (Optional)

The actual process of baking bread is not time consuming, but the stages are. If you don't have a mixer of any sort you can do this by hand. It has been done that way for hundreds of years. If you choose to do it by hand, be prepared to get your back into it. Kneading dough by hand requires ten minutes of non-stop pounding and pushing and pulling.

1. In the mixing bowl, dissolve the yeast in the water with the sugar. Stir to dissolve. Let it sit for about 10-20 minutes.

2. This would be a good time to chop the rosemary.

3. When the yeast mixture becomes a little foamy, stir in the salt.

4. Slowly add in the flour as you beat on low speed.

5. Once all of the flour has been combined, knead at high speed for about 8-10 minutes. You may need to keep a hand on the top of the mixer. At high speed they tend to walk around a bit on the counter top.

6. In the last minute or so add the rosemary and olive oil. If you don't like the taste of rosemary you could substitute olives or garlic, or nothing at all. The dough will be ready when it is sticky, and is all wrapped around the hook and not in the bowl.

7. Remove the bowl from the mixer stand, place it in a warm place and cover with a clean dish towel.

8. Let the dough sit for about two and a half hours to rise. It should become about twice its size.

9. Shake a layer of cornstarch onto a pizza peel. If you don't have a pizza peel, you can use parchment or wax paper. You want something that isn't going to stick to your very sticky dough.

10. Remove the dough with a rubber spatula (or your fingers) onto the peel. Form it into a rectangular loaf. Don't worry, it will not look particularly pretty at this point.

11. Cover with a clean dish towel and let sit for about another ½ hour.

12. Pre heat the oven with the pizza stone in it to 500°. If you are using a cookie sheet, pre heat it instead.

13. Carefully slide the loaf onto the stone. You may need a pastry knife or large spatula to scrape a little. If you are using a cookie sheet, carefully remove it with mitts or double towels, place it on the stovetop and slide or flip the loaf onto it. Carefully place it back in the oven.

14. There is an old trick that you can spray or flick water onto the bottom of the oven several times in the first five minutes. This will help the outside of the bread become crisp. I also know of people placing an oven proof cup or small container of water in with it to create steam. None of these things are really necessary, but do it if you feel like it. I spray water with a spray bottle. Be warned though, I did this once, carelessly spraying the water in an old oven and blew out the light bulb all into the dough, ruining my bread.

15. The bread should turn a golden brown after about 10 minutes.

16. Turn the oven down to 325º at this point and continue baking for about another 20 minutes.

17. Thump on the bread at this point. It should sound hollow.

Remove to a wire baking rack and let sit for at least one hour, longer if you can stand it. The bread will continue to cook on the inside as it sits and cools. This bread will last most of the week in a sealed plastic bag. If any of it actually lasts that long, make some croutons.

# THE FRITTATA BASICS

The Frittata is the Italian cross between a quiche and an omelette. Like both of these French egg dishes, the Frittata's main function is to make the best use of what's in the fridge. It does not have a crust but is served like a pie. The preparation is simple and, provided that you have a few eggs, the ingredients are based entirely on what is at hand.

An important factor in making a frittata is the equipment. I used to own two identical non-stick crepe pans. This worked very well as I could cook one side and then flip from one pan to the other to cook the other side. Now I use a non-stick pan and a very large pancake spatula for flipping. For the brave, just the non-stick and a deft flick of the wrist will also do. If this is your preferred method, some practice before trying this in front of friends is recommended. There is another method where the mostly cooked frittata is slid onto a large, flat plate and the pan is placed on top, carefully flipped and the plate slid away.

If you have a broiler in your oven, you can cook the bottom on the stovetop and finish by browning the top in the broiler. This works well if you have an ovenproof pan. Most non-stick pans cannot go in the oven so make sure that you read the manufacturers information carefully before ruining your pan and your breakfast.

Regardless of the non-stickiness of the pan, I still recommend you use some sort of fat to further grease the way. Cooking some bacon in the pan prior to the egg dish works really well and gives you the first ingredient for your frittata, or you can use olive oil or butter or any combination.

1. Get the pan hot and prepare the grease.

2. In a mixing bowl, crack the eggs and whip them with a whisk. It is important for a light frittata to get as much air in the eggs as possible.

3. Add a bit of pepper and chopped up leftovers.

4. If the recipe that you have chosen has a hard cheese like parmesan, I suggest that you leave out the salt for now. There is enough salt in the cheese for the cooking process.

5. Whip the leftovers with the eggs and pour into a non-stick (6" or 8") pan.

6. Over med high heat cook the egg mixture without moving it for 5 to 10 minutes. Cover to cook the top too.

7. Flip and cook for a few minutes on the other side or uncover and place under the broiler to finish the top.

In the below recipes I use 4 or 5 eggs. You can make a frittata with as little as 2 eggs. I suggest the smaller pan for this size. Amazingly, you can have leftovers from leftovers! It also goes along with my theory that you never know when you end up needing to feed a second person. It's nice to have to take to a neighbor or have for lunch with a salad. Unlike omelettes, frittatas can last for a day or two in the refrigerator.

This morning I fixed one for my son and his friend. Here it is:

# STIR FRY FRITTATA

My particular stir-fry from the night before contained chicken, baby broccoli, mushrooms, onions, peppers and shallots.

## INGREDIENTS
**5 Eggs**
**Bacon Grease**
**1/4 Cup Parmesan Cheese**
**Chopped Italian Parsley (For Garnish)**
**1/2 Cup Stir Fry Chicken and Vegetables Leftovers**

## TOOLS
**Chef's Knife**
**Cutting Board**
**Whisk (or Fork)**
**Mixing Bowl**
**Non-Stick Pan**

1. Whip the eggs with a whisk in a medium bowl

2. Add pepper and the stir-fry leftovers.

3. Add half of the cheese.

4. Pour into hot, greased non-stick pan.

5. Cook over med high heat for about ten minutes, taking care not to burn the bottom. Cover while cooking to aid in the cooking of the top.

6. When just congealed flip. You will only need to cook the other side for a few minutes. I suggest flipping back to the lighter side to serve.

Garnish with the rest of the cheese and parsley. I even use leftover parsley. Whenever I chop parsley I put what I don't use in a small plastic bag. Make sure you use it in a day or two. The whole point of using Italian Parsley is for the freshness that it imparts to the dish.

The best part of the frittata is that it will keep in the refrigerator for two or three days. I think it is wonderful the next day. Remove it from the fridge about 20 minutes before you are ready to eat. It is so good room temperature. Before you refrigerate make sure to scrape off any garnishes such as herbs or tomatoes. Chop fresh when you serve it next and you will have a whole new frittata experience.

## OTHER GREAT FRITTATA LEFTOVER IDEAS

Steak
Lamb
Chicken
Grilled Vegetables
Pasta
Grilled or Fried Potatoes
Sausages
Mushrooms
Olives
Cheese
Bacon

# PROSCIUTTO AND CHEDDAR FRITTATA

## INGREDIENTS
5 Eggs
1 Tablespoon Butter
4-6 Pieces Prosciutto, chopped (Or any cured ham)
1/4 Cup Shredded Cheddar Cheese
Chopped Fresh Herbs (Italian Parsley, Chives, Thyme)
8-10 Cherry Tomatoes, Sliced in Half

## TOOLS
Chef's Knife
Cutting Board
Whisk (or Fork)
Mixing Bowl
Non-Stick Pan

1. Whip the eggs with a whisk in a medium bowl.

2. Add pepper, cheese and the prosciutto.

3. Melt the butter in a non-stick pan.

4. Pour egg mixture into the pan.

5. Cook over med high heat for about ten minutes, taking care not to burn the bottom. Cover while cooking to aid in the cooking of the top.

6. If you have an oven proof, non stick then place it under the broiler for about 5 minutes to finish cooking the top.

Slide the finished frittata onto a large, flat plate or serving platter. Arrange the tomatoes on top then sprinkle with the chopped herbs. Cut like a pie.

## DESSERT

For most people born into western civilization, a sweet tooth is a nurtured and prized (if not guilty) pleasure. I try to refrain from the more obvious and empty calories found in snickers bars and soft serve ice cream.

It is so easy to wander down the center isles of the grocery and buy a tub of chemical ice cream or a bag of cookies with the shelf life of two millennia and call that dessert. Rest assured, if you are shopping for an evening in by yourself you are guaranteed to eat the whole tub of "Ice Cream" or slowly and absent-mindedly nibble your way through the entire bag of "Cookies".

As I often say, you can never hurt yourself if you stay on the perimeter (of the grocery). Buy fruit. It is not expensive, it's good for you and you can make a variety of great desserts with fruit as the main ingredient.

# PEACHES THREE WAYS

## BELLINI

The original Bellini was invented at Harry's Bar in Venice. Leave it to the Italians to come up with the most delicious cocktail ever. The recipe is universally well known and only varies in the fruit used and the ratio between fruit juice and prosecco.

White Peaches are the original fruit used at Harry's Bar and the single best version of this I have ever had was at the River Café in London. They also used white peaches. If you can't find white peaches you can use yellow peaches or white nectarines. Regardless of the fruit you use, they need to be very ripe and sweet. There are other cocktails made with sparkling wine but they are not bellinis.

This is not exactly a dessert, in fact just the opposite, but it is a great Sunday drink. Have it for dessert if you would like.

### INGREDIENTS
**6-8 Ripe White Peaches**
**1 bottle of Prosecco or Cava or other Sparkling Wine**

### TOOLS
**Juicer (any kind will do)**
**Fine Strainer**

1. Squeeze the juice out of the peaches. I use a simple wooden hand juicer. Anything will work, as the peaches should be so ripe that you can practically squeeze the juice out with your hand. Use a juicer or a food processor to get the most out of them, though.

2. Once you squeeze the juice out, strain it through a fine strainer.

3. Refrigerate the juice. The key to making a great bellini is making sure that both the peach juice and the sparkling wine are REALLY cold.

4. The ratio that I prefer is 1/3 peach juice to 2/3 wine. Fill a champagne flute with 2/3 prosecco and then slowly pour in the peach juice. Sounds simple but I guarantee that you will love it.

## GRILLED PEACHES

This is still not strictly dessert. I often serve these as a second side dish, but they can also be served as dessert.

**INGREDIENTS**
**1-2 Peaches (or donut peaches if you can find them)**
**Olive Oil**
**Ground Pepper**
**Powdered Sugar (Optional)**

**TOOLS**
**Chef's Knife**
**Cutting Board**
**Grill or Grill pan**

1. Cut the peaches in half and remove the stone.

2. Slice the peaches in ¼" thick rounds.

3. Lightly drizzle or brush with olive oil on both sides to keep from sticking to the grill. You can skip the oil if you have a non-stick grill pan.

4. Grill the peaches on both sides for about three or four minutes each. You still want the peaches to be a bit firm, not goopy and falling apart.

5. Grind some black pepper over them.

6. Serve over ice cream or dusted with powdered sugar. I will sometimes skip the pepper if I am going to have them with the powdered sugar, although they are great either way.

## PEPPERED PEACHES

Here is an actual dessert recipe. Kirk Francis taught me about this over the phone one hot summer night.

**INGREDIENTS**
**1-2 Ripe Peaches, sliced into thin wedges, stone removed**
**¼ Cup Balsamic Vinegar (use the cheap one, not the 50 year old one)**
**¼ Cup Sugar**
**Ground Black Pepper**

**TOOLS**
**Chef's Knife**
**Cutting Board**
**Small Mixing Bowl (with cover if you have one)**

1.  Slice the peaches into pretty thin pieces and place in the bowl.

2.  Mix in the sugar and vinegar.

3.  Liberally pepper and mix a little more.

4.  Cover and refrigerate for at least 2 hours. 8 hours is perfect.

Serve over (homemade) ice cream, pound cake, or just with a little whipped cream. This same treatment works well for strawberries.

# HOMEMADE ICE CREAM

Even though I am lactose intolerant, I loved homemade ice cream when I was a kid. It was lots of hard work for my neighbor Ed Ottenga, who would hand-crank homemade ice cream at least once a summer. I know it was hard work because I would get my turn on the crank.

Today, this process has been made a lot easier by the small, affordable ice cream machine. The old machines were messy – requiring lots of rock salt and ice that went everywhere – and took a really long time. The new machine has an ingenious insulated bowl that is first frozen in the freezer then placed on the machine. The ingredients are added and the machine churns on the counter top for 20 or 30 minutes and then magically you have ice cream. I am not big on kitchen gadgets, but this one is well worth the money.

# BAKING

Bananas are really good and really good for you. Personally, I hate them once they go the slightest bit soft. I have thrown away more bananas than I have ever consumed. A couple of weeks ago, while on my own in New York, I thought that I would finally do what I always say I was going to do with the rotting bananas: Bake bread.

Although I do love baking the occasional loaf of bread, I do not consider myself a baker. It generally involves more science and less improvising than my culinary desires and constricted time allow. My wife bakes. I watch her with amazement as she talks on the phone, yells at the kids and somehow, with one hand, out of the corner of her eye, bakes and ices a cake, or whips up a batch of cookies "from scratch". And this is not a woman who multi-tasks easily.

I finally realized what it is about baking that makes it relatively easy for her. It is the same every time. There is no "A pinch of this, maybe a bit more of that". The recipe is not a suggestion, it is a formula. Two cups of sugar, one cup of flour, two eggs, teaspoon of salt, teaspoon of vanilla, 1/2 cup nuts...You do that every time and an hour later out comes some amazing baked goods, all incredibly different and delicious and seemingly from the exact same ingredients.

So when I did some research as to how to make this bread from rotting bananas, what I discovered was forty different "recipes" with exactly the same "formula". So, needless to say, the following recipe is not exactly original.

The Banana Nut Bread formula realized.

## BANANA NUT BREAD (The Formula)

<u>**INGREDIENTS**</u>
**2 Cups Flour**
**1 Cup Sugar**
**1/2 Cup (4 oz) Butter (or other fat of some sort)**
**2 Eggs**
**1 Teaspoon Baking Soda (not the one open in the fridge to absorb odors)**
**2-3 Bananas that you wouldn't eat but aren't completely black – smashed up**
**1/2 Cup Walnuts or Pecans, chopped**

<u>**TOOLS**</u>
**Non-Stick Loaf Pan**
**Mixing Bowl**

1. Pre heat the oven to 325º.

2. Mix all of these ingredients together until you have a smooth batter. Some might tell you to mix the sugar and butter first. The important thing is that you get it all mixed up. You can use a hand mixer but I just use a fork.

3. Pour the mixture into a buttered and very lightly floured, non-stick pan. This can be a loaf pan or whatever you have that looks like it will hold the amount of batter you have. The baking soda will make it rise slightly so allow room for that.

4. Cook for about an hour and 15 minutes. The old test is to stick a toothpick or knife into the middle and if it comes out clean then the bread is cooked all the way through. If you cook it for 85 minutes at anywhere near 325 it WILL be cooked all the way through. Don't get to crazy about this.

## VARIATIONS

The first four ingredients are always the same ratio. You can make any kind of sweet bread using this formula. The Baking soda gives it a bit of lift. You could also use baking powder. You can add flavor and texture with anything that you can think of. This is the baking equivalent of pizza or a frittata. It's perfect for things that you have had a bit too long, especially fruit. You could use peaches or pears or even apples. Add any nuts for texture. Dried fruits like dates and apricots would also make a nice, sweet bread.

My point is that although baking is a science, and therefore you CAN and should experiment. In this case, the formula remains consistent and just the flavor accents change. As long as you stick to the formula you will have something delicious and creative, guaranteed.

You can also make cupcakes using the same batter.

# CHOCOLATE CHIP COOKIES

Just like the banana nut bread, chocolate chip cookies are another simple formula. Once you can make this basic cookie you are on your way to whatever cookie your heart desires. I like to bake a batch on Sunday and have them to dip in my coffee all week long.

**INGREDIENTS**
**2 ¼ Cups All-Purpose, Unbleached Flour**
**1 ¾ Cups Sugar**
**2 Eggs**
**2 Sticks Butter**
**1 Bag Chocolate Chips (or Butterscotch)**
**2 Teaspoons Vanilla**
**1 Teaspoon Salt**
**1 Teaspoon Baking Soda**

**TOOLS**
**Mixing Bowl**
**Hand Mixer (optional)**
**Cookie Sheet**
**Fine Strainer**
**Cookie Jar (optional, but why don't you have a cookie jar?)**

1. Sit the eggs and butter on the counter to get to room temperature. Give them an hour or so.

2. Pre-heat the oven to 375º.

3. Sift the flour through the strainer.

4. Add the rest of the dry ingredients.

5. In another bowl, mix the butter and sugar into a cream.

6. Add one egg at a time.

7. Add the vanilla.

8. Slowly beat in the dry ingredients and the chocolate chips.

9. Scoop golf ball size balls onto a non-stick or buttered cookie sheet.

10. Bake 8-10 minutes.

11. Repeat until all of the batter is gone.

Should make about 3 dozen cookies.

# Chapter 11
## DATE NIGHT

Many of you are young and single. Even if you aren't, you may be faced with this sort of challenge in your culinary repertoire. Living on your own, you are likely to want or have to have someone over for a meal.  Maybe you may even want to have a few people over. The ideas in this chapter can be expanded to have a small dinner party. Just use the ratios and expand as needed. The process and time will essentially be the same.

So far, you have done pretty well for yourself. You have prepared several meals and enjoyed them. You've even made a soup and turned some leftovers into amazing pasta. You are starting to feel cocky about your new found prowess in the kitchen. Hold on there, chef, don't get too carried away.

Preparing a meal for someone that you would like to impress comes with a whole new set of considerations. I have included some recipes that can be prepared for two that don't leave you in the kitchen panicking instead of enjoying a glass of champagne together or sharing a sunset from your balcony.

The key to cooking for someone else, especially someone that you might like, is that you want your cooking to appear like it is effortless. I have friends that have been having me to dinner for years. I am always impressed with the minimal amount of cooking that they actually do when I am there. The food always seems to miraculously appear when it is time to eat.

But, as by now you have discovered, no cooking is effortless. And you might think that one of the recipes that you have already made would be great to share with someone else. I even said earlier that there is enough for two in many of these dishes, just in case someone drops by. But I have thought of the following recipes specifically to appear effortless. You should be able to do most everything ahead of time and only be left with some small, last minute tasks and an impressive presentation.

You have to do two things ahead of time. You need to properly plan, leaving plenty of time for shopping and preparation and you need to invite someone that you like and who will appreciate your effort. What happens after that is also up to you, but does not fall within the parameters of this book.

You will notice that I have given you guidelines about how much total time it will take - broken down into the preparation time (before your date shows up); cooking time (during when your date shows up); and last minute labor. The "cooking time" for these particular dishes requires little, if any participation. The "last minute labor" is always meant to be short and simple.

## ROASTED CHICKEN

Prep Time: :30 minutes
Cooking Time: 1:30
Last Minute Labor: 5 minutes, minimal labor

There are so many things that are so perfect about this dish I don't know where to start. First of all, this is comfort food at it's finest. Second, this dish can be made totally in advance. The only real last minute labor is pulling it out of the oven and letting it rest for a few minutes before you serve it. Third, the whole meal is cooked in one pan, so if you do a tiny amount of cleaning as you go, the kitchen will be spotless.

Buy a smallish whole chicken, about three to five pounds. Get an organic one if you can. Make sure it looks and smells fresh. Do not buy the cheapest one. That would be really impressive, your date going home with food poisoning.

### INGREDIENTS
**Small Roasting Chicken**
**5-6 Small Red or New Potatoes**
**1 Lemon**
**1 White Onion**
**2 Large Carrots**
**1 Fennel Bulb**
**1 Cup of Chicken Broth**
**Sprigs of Fresh Rosemary and Thyme**
**Olive Oil**
**Salt and Pepper**

### TOOLS
**Roasting pan (Pyrex is good)**
**Chef's Knife**
**String**

1. Pre-heat the oven to 350º. Make sure there is a rack in the center of the oven or one slot below and nothing above it.

2. Cut all of the vegetables and the potatoes into bite size chunks, roughly 1" squares.

3. Cut the lemon into quarters.

4. Remove any of the organs that have been conveniently stuffed in the carcass.

5. Thoroughly wash the chicken inside and out. Tap it dry with paper towels.

6. Rub it with a light amount of olive oil inside and out and salt and pepper.

7. Stuff the inside with a few chunks of lemon and onion and the whole sprigs of rosemary and thyme.

8. Tie the legs together with string so the stuffing doesn't fall out. This is actually not that big of a deal so don't make it a production. If you can't find a piece of string then skip it.

9. Place the potatoes, carrots, fennel and the rest of the onion on the bottom of the roasting pan, creating a bed for the chicken to sit on.

10. Sit the chicken on top of the vegetables, breast side up.

11. Pour about half of the chicken broth in the bottom. Save the other half to add if it starts to dry out.

12. Place the pan on the center rack of your pre-heated oven and cook for about an hour and a half, or 18 minutes per pound, depending on the size of the bird and the consistency of your oven. I suggest that you try this once before you have your date, noting the size of the chicken and the time that it took. Generally, when you cut into the bit between the leg and the breast the liquid should be clear. If not, put the bird back in for another 10 – 15 minutes. If you would like to test this with an instant read thermometer, remove the chicken from the oven and take a reading in the thickest part of the breast or thigh, making sure not to touch a bone. The reading after 15 seconds should be 175-180.

13. Once the chicken is cooked, remove it from the oven and let it sit for 5 – 10 minutes, loosely covered with some foil. This period of rest lets the chicken relax and will make for a much more moist and tender meat.

Here is the only bit of post preparation that you need to make. If you are feeling confident of your carving skills, you can simply place the roasting pan on a trivet directly on the table and serve from there. Or, you can transfer the bird to a serving platter and garnish it with the potatoes and vegetables, or lastly you can carve the chicken in the kitchen, laying the pieces on a platter with the potatoes and vegetables. Remember, the idea is that you are presenting a delicious dinner with as little time spent in the kitchen as possible. If you haven't ever carved a chicken before then you should practice before your date.

## STEAK AND POTATOES

Prep Time: :30 minutes
Cooking time: 1 hour
Last Minute Labor: 10 minutes

As my friend Kirk would say, "any stupid republican can grill a steak." The "angry steak" recipe below is stolen from his cookbook. The preparation of this particular steak is really easy and has an impressive result. Because of it's thickness, the cooking time is minimal, making it the perfect date meal.

Make sure that your date eats red meat before you commit to this menu. I know you are saying to yourself that steak, a baked potato and salad is not a very impressive meal, but like the roasted chicken, it is comfort food and the variation on this steak, along with how really easy you are going to make it look makes it the perfect date meal. The only downside to this as a date meal is all of the garlic. The old adage is that if you both eat the garlic then one cancels out the other. That's my story and I'm sticking to it.

There are only four tasks that you need to perform in front of your date: cooking the steak, removing the potatoes from the oven, dressing the salad and laying out the condiments for the potatoes. Everything else will be done ahead of time.

## INGREDIENTS
2 Sirloin Steaks, Fairly Thin
2 Russet Potatoes
Bunch of Lettuce
1 Red Pepper
5 Cloves of Garlic, Minced
Red Pepper Flakes
5-6 Button Mushrooms
Bunch of Green Onions or Chives
Small Container Sour Cream
1 Stick of Butter
Olive Oil
Red Wine Vinegar

## TOOLS
Salad bowl
Mixing bowl
Grill or Grill Pan
Small Tupperware container with lid (or jar)
2 Ramekins or other small bowls
Chef's Knife

1. Wash and dry the lettuce and place it in the salad bowl.

2. Clean and chop the mushrooms and the red pepper into bite size pieces and add them to the bowl.

3. Gently toss with your <u>clean</u> hands.

4. Place a very slightly damp paper towel on top of the bowl and put it in the refrigerator. The paper towel helps to keep the salad fresh and crisp. You can do this up to 4 hours before you serve it.

5. In a Tupperware container or a jar that has a lid or even a cup, combine 2 tablespoons vinegar and 6 tablespoons olive oil.

6. Add 1 clove of minced garlic, a pinch of sea salt and a twist or two of ground pepper and whisk together.

7. Stick the lid on or cover with plastic wrap and refrigerate.

8. Clean the green onions, removing the very tip of the white end.

9. Chop the white part, through the light green part and about an inch into the dark green. You want to end up with approximately even amounts of all three.

10. Put this into a little bowl, cover and refrigerate.

11. In a mixing bowl, combine approximately four tablespoons of olive oil, 3 cloves of minced garlic and 1 teaspoon of red pepper flakes.

12. Take one of the steaks and put it in a large plastic bag.

13. With a heavy cup or Pyrex measuring cup or wooden rolling pin (there is a tool for this but it is totally not necessary) pound the steak until it is at least half the thickness that it started.

14. Stick into the bowl and coat both sides with the marinade.

15. Do the same with the other steak.

16. Cover and refrigerate.

17. Pre heat the oven to 375º.

18. Wrap the potatoes in aluminium foil and poke several holes in them with a fork.

19. Place on the middle rack of the oven and bake for an hour.

20. Remove the steak from the refrigerator 10 - 15 minutes before you are going to cook it.

21. Start the grill (if you have propane, this should take about the 5 minutes to get up to temperature, coals take longer). If you are using a grill pan (or even a regular pan) get it hot over a med high flame. Since the steak has been soaking in olive oil, there is no need for any additional fat in the pan.

22. The steak should take 5 minutes or less per side depending on how angry you were when you were beating it and how you and your guest like it cooked. If either like it rare, then this was probably the wrong dish to make. The steak is so thin that is cooks very quickly.

23. Remove the steak onto a plate and let it rest for five minutes.

24. While it rests, remove the salad, the green onions, the dressing, the sour cream and butter from the refrigerator.

25. Shake or stir the dressing and toss the salad with it, adding just enough to lightly coat the leaves of lettuce.

26. Put some sour cream in another small bowl and put the butter, sour cream and green onions on the table with serving spoons for each.

27. Remove the potatoes from the oven and take the foil off. Foil has a unique property that it does not get very hot in the oven so you can actually (quickly) remove it with your bare hands.

I would serve the salad in separate bowls or directly from the salad bowl, and serve the steak and potato on another plate. Enjoy!

# LAMB SHANKS

Prep time: 30 minutes
Cooking time: 3 hours
Finishing time: 5 minutes

I learned to cook lamb shanks from Sally Schmidt, original chef and owner of the French Laundry. Sally, like all of the California fresh food pioneers, emphasized the ingredients being really fresh and in season. This is a wintertime dish and perfect for a fire in the fireplace and a delicious, hearty red wine. I'll leave dessert up to you.

There is another, very similar recipe in this book. This is my 'date night' variation. Make sure that you ask your date if he or she eats lamb.

This is a perfect date recipe as ALL of the preparation is done well ahead of time. You might want to do this on a weekend because of the cooking time. I made this the other night though and didn't start shopping until 5, so it is possible to do in the evening if you have practiced it once or twice.

A dutch oven is a wonderful thing. They are cast iron, old fashioned and just the most amazing devices - simple and efficient and well worth the purchase. They sometimes go on sale, too. If you don't have one, a covered, ovenproof pan or casserole will work just fine. The idea is that you need something that can work on the stovetop for sautéing and browning then transfer to the oven for cooking. If you don't have any of these, you can always cover a sauté pan with aluminium foil.

## INGREDIENTS
2 Good Sized Lamb Shanks
1 Onion, Chopped
2 Large Carrots, Chopped
1 Fennel Bulb, Chopped
Handful of Small Potatoes, Cut in half when necessary to make all the same size
2 Garlic Cloves, Minced
1 Cup Red Wine
2 Cups Chicken or Beef Broth or Water
Mint or Rosemary
Bay Leaf
1 Lemon

## TOOLS
Dutch Oven or Ovenproof Casserole with Lid
Chef's knife
Chopping Board

1. Pre heat the oven to 350º.

2. Squeeze one lemon over the shanks, salt and pepper, then let sit for a few minutes.

3. Chop the vegetables.

4. On the stove top, heat a tablespoon or so of olive oil in the dutch oven.

5. Add the shanks and let them brown. Don't rush this. Let them sit on each side for a few minutes.

6. Remove the shanks.

7.   Deglaze the pan with a glug of wine.

8.  Add a bit more olive oil and a pat of butter, scrape the left over shank's brown bits off the bottom.

9.  Add the onion and garlic and sauté.

10. When translucent, add the other vegetables and potatoes.

11. Salt and Pepper.

12. Sauté for a few minutes.

13. Place the Shanks back on top of the vegetables and add the liquid to cover.

14. Spoon a few of the potatoes and vegetables over the shanks.

15. Add a few sprigs of mint or rosemary and a bay leaf.

16. Put the cover on the dutch oven and place in the oven. Be careful, it's hot!

17. Let this cook for about 3 hours. The meat should be falling off the bone.

Serving this meal is really easy. Place each shank carefully on a plate and spoon over the potatoes and vegetables.

A word about lamb shanks: Not all groceries always carry them. Call ahead.

# BAKED SALMON WITH RICE AND ASPARAGUS SALAD

Prep time: 20 minutes
Cooking time: 30 minutes
Finishing time: 10 minutes

Baking salmon is simple and elegant. The preparation for this dish is simple and quick. The Asparagus salad makes this meal creative and different without any hassle or gamble. This meal is dependent on three really good quality, fresh ingredients: wild caught salmon (make sure the fillet has no bones); really fresh, large asparagus; really good parmesan cheese. I suggest you really splurge for the last ingredient. The parmesan should be nutty and slightly salty. Find a cheese or other specialty shop and ask for their very best. A big hunk will cost you about ten dollars.

## INGREDIENTS
**1 Med. Wild Caught Salmon Fillet (Enough for Two)**
**1 Lemon**
**1 Cup Long Grain Rice (Brown or White)**
**1 Bunch Really Fresh Large Asparagus**
**1 Tablespoon Minced Fresh Ginger**
**Olive Oil**
**Really Good Parmesan**
**Balsamic Vinegar**
**Sea Salt**
**Ground White Pepper (Optional)**

## TOOLS
**Pyrex baking dish**
**Med. Pan**
**Mandolin (optional)**
**Hand Peeler**
**Chef's Knife**
**Chopping Board**

The first thing that you need to do is to double check that the salmon has no bones. Run your (clean) fingers along the ridge of the fillet and feel for the pointy tops of any leftover bones. If you find them, use some tweezers or clean needle nose pliers to carefully remove. Pull straight out, trying not to remove or destroy too much of the flesh.

1. Cut the hard ends off the asparagus and soak them in a large bowl of iced water for 20 minutes. The hard end is usually about 2 inches in or You can test this by bending and see where it breaks naturally.

2. The timing of this meal depends on the rice. Please check the rice package for exact details. Usually rice takes 30 – 45 minutes.

3. Pre-heat the oven to 325º.

4. Mince the ginger.

5. Slice 4-5 very thin slices of lemon.

6. Put the salmon in the dish, very lightly drizzle it with olive oil and squeeze the rest of the lemon over it.

7. Sprinkle the ginger evenly, lightly salt and pepper (white pepper if you have it) and top with the lemon slices.

8. Place on the middle rack of the oven for 25-30 minutes.

9. Dry the asparagus with a bunch of paper towels.

10. If you have a mandolin, very thinly slice the asparagus lengthwise. You should end up with paper-thin arrow shaped asparagus. If you don't have a mandolin, thinly slice lengthwise with a sharp knife.

11. Cover with a slightly damp paper towel and refrigerate.

12. With a peeler, shave a good deal of parmesan onto a plate and set aside.

13. When the rice and Salmon are cooked, turn the rice off.

14. The rice should sit for 10 minutes.

15. Whenever the salmon is finished, sit it on top of the stove. It can sit for 5-10 minutes.

Cut the salmon in half, spoon the rice onto a plate and cover with the salmon. On the side of the plate or on a separate salad plate, artistically layer the sliced asparagus and cheese, drizzle with a little olive oil and a few drops of good balsamic vinegar. If you really want to gild the lilly, add a few drops of truffle oil.

# STIR FRY SHRIMP

Prep time: 30 minutes
Cooking time:  30 minutes
Finishing time: 15 minutes

This is a little more cooking in front of your guest than the other recipes so far, but the process is really simple and can be fun to watch.

## INGREDIENTS
½ lb. Uncooked, Cleaned and De-Veined Lrg. Shrimp (15-20)
2 Heads Baby Bok Choy, Rough Chopped
2 Carrots, Chopped
2 Celery Stalks, Chopped
1 Cup Mushrooms (Crimini, Shitake or any others)
1 Granny Smith Apple, Chopped
½ Cup Snow Peas
½ Red Pepper, Chopped
1 Bunch Green Onions, Cleaned And Chopped
2 Garlic Cloves, Minced
1 Tablespoon Fresh Ginger, Minced
1 Small Bunch Cilantro (Chopped) (Optional)
Soy Sauce
2 Ounces Oyster Sauce
1 Tablespoon Rice Wine Vinegar
1 Cup Rice (White or Brown)
2 Tablespoons Vegetable Oil
1 Small Jalapeño Pepper, Deseeded And Minced

## Tools
Large Pan or Wok
Chef's Knife
Chopping Board
1 Med Sauce Pan

1.  Chop all of the vegetables ahead of time. If you want to look like a tv chef you can put each in it's own little bowl. You can also put them in plastic bags in the fridge, or reverse layer most of them into one bowl, with the softer vegetables on the bottom and the harder ones on top. Keep the garlic and onion separate.

2.  Remove the tail and any other not so nice things and wash the shrimp. Pat them dry and store them in a sealed container in the refrigerator until you are ready to cook.

3.  Start the rice. It takes 30-45 minutes. You can cook all of the stir fry in the last 15 minutes or so. The rice will also need to sit for another 10 minutes so keep this in mind.

4.  In a large pan or wok, heat the oil.

5.  Add the garlic, ginger and onions and sauté.

6.  Add the vegetables, hard ones to soft ones and sauté. All should only need to cook for 10 minutes or so. Make room as you go by pushing the more cooked vegetables up the side, out of the way, to make room on the bottom for the new ones.

7.  Cook the shrimp last. Once everything is cooked stir in the vinegar, oyster sauce and a few drizzles of soy sauce.

8.  Cook for another 2-3 minutes to let the sauce thoroughly coat all of the shrimp and veg.

Serve over the rice.

# Chapter 12
## CLEAN UP

      That's right, the horrible task that you would do anything to get out of when you were a kid. There is no question about it: washing dishes is a pain in the butt. But, if you are cooking on your own, you are going to create some dirty dishes. Unless you have a daily maid service, you are going to have to deal with them. I have a few suggestions that might make this a quicker, easier and (relatively) painless task.

# PREPARATION

Your first chance to make the cleaning life easier is to not make a mess in the first place. When you watch Bobby Flay or any of the other TV Chefs du jour, they have all of their ingredients already prepared in neat little ramekins or some other beautifully arranged little bowls. Rest assured that someone else has prepped those ingredients and will clean them up after they disappear out of the view of the camera.

In real life, try not to use too many of anything. Proper preparation is the key to well-timed, successful cooking but you are not shooting a cooking show.

For example: if you are chopping vegetables that all go into the same dish at the same time, put them into one bowl or directly into the pot or pan. If you are preparing ingredients that have a particular sequence, and there is time in between the cooking process, prep them in order. If a particular dish requires sautéed garlic, then sautéed onions, then mushrooms, etc in that order then chop the garlic first, transfer it from the chopping board to the pan, wipe the board and chop the onion, add directly to the pan, wash the same board and cut the mushrooms. There is no reason to use dishes or disposable plates or foil or anything else to hold the ingredients before they go into the pan.

Before you start to cook, take five minutes to plan, either on paper or in your head. Think about what processes you will need to perform, what order you will do things, when each of these tasks will be performed, and what tools and dishes you will need. Cooking is like dancing or playing music. Timing is everything and rehearsal is essential.

## POTS AND PANS

There are recipes in this book that use just one pan. Just like the preparation, think about your process when you decide what pots and pans to use. I include a list of the tools needed with each recipe and I always try to keep them to a minimum. You should do the same thing as you prepare meals on your own.

## CLEAN AS YOU GO

There are two reasons why you should try to clean your tools as you go. First of all, they will be clean and not piled up when the meal is over. After you have had a delicious meal and have made your way through the better part of a bottle of wine, the last thing you want to do is to wash a big pile of pots and pans. The second and more important reason is that it is much easier and sometimes necessary for the preservation of your tools.

**WOOD** – In my kitchen, there is a great deal of wood. Among my often used wooden tools are a cutting board, stirring spoons, citrus juicer, pizza peel and salad bowl. There are some special considerations when cleaning these tools. First is that they must be cleaned as soon as they are used. Wood is porous and if left to sit for a while tends to hold onto the taste and smell of what was last on it. When food has a chance to dry on wood it requires either soaking or scrubbing, both of which are bad for wood. Too much soap is also bad for wood. Like food, the taste of soap tends to get soaked up into the wood if overexposed. And I personally do not like the taste of soap.

**SAUTÉ PANS** – When you sauté meat or chicken or anything else that sticks, you end up with a mess. There is a common cooking method called "Deglazing" that creates a delicious sauce made by reducing some sort of acidic liquid such as vinegar or wine in the pan with the drippings. This loosens the stuff stuck to the bottom of the pan and combines it with the liquid. The result is a nice sauce and a clean pan. Deglazing is a great way of making a sauce.

This same technique can be used to clean the sticky stuff off the bottom of the pan. Instead of wine, add a little water and some gentle heat and you can "deglaze" your way to a clean pan. You will still need to wash it with hot water and soap afterwards, but you won't have to scrape and scrub, cutting your cleaning time by more than half and saving a considerable amount of elbow grease. Make sure to let the pan cool before you wash it.

**DISHES, PLATES, FLATWARE** – I used to be of the school that the kitchen and all of it's contents needed to be cleaned and put away directly after a meal. I certainly still like this because I like to wake up to a clean kitchen – it's like a clean slate. But, I no longer force myself do this if I don't feel like it, or it will interrupt something else important, like reading a good book, or watching reruns of Jeopardy.

If I have cleaned my tools as I go, there is very little left to do. I have discovered a couple of things over the years. If you let things soak a little bit they are much easier to rinse before you put them in the dishwasher or wash them by hand. I have also discovered that if you leave a few dishes for the morning that you won't be arrested and hauled off to dirty kitchen jail. These days I get up, put the coffee on and, while it is brewing, clean what I left from the night before. This is really no big deal, it let's me enjoy the evening without ending a relaxing meal with more work and it gives me something to do while the coffee is brewing.

I don't suggest leaving dirty dishes for very long, especially if you have any kind of pests like roaches, but a few dishes and plates soaking in the sink overnight will not reek havoc in most civilized living situations.

**SAFETY** – I have a couple of plastic cutting boards that I only use for chicken and meat. They are two different colors so I remember which one is for which. I wash chicken into a clean, empty sink and transfer it to the chicken board. I use paper towels to dry the chicken and use the board to trim and or cut the bird if necessary. I prepare the chicken on that board or on a plate and wash my hands with soap and hot water both before and after handling the chicken. I wash the board and also put it in the dishwasher. (dishwashers only sanitize dishes, they do not actually wash them) I wash the knife with very hot water and soap. Anything that comes into contact with the raw chicken gets washed and then goes into the dishwasher if it can (never put your good knifes in the dishwasher). The last part of this chicken safety ritual is that I through all of the wrappers, paper towels, etc directly into the exterior garbage and thoroughly wash the sink. Most chicken is perfectly safe, but uncooked chicken can carry with it some pretty nasty bacteria. There is no reason to take a chance.

Beef and pork get pretty much the same treatment, although I usually do not wash meat before preparing it. Unlike chicken, meat and pork are cleaned, and chopped into different cuts before being sold. (Always thoroughly wash chicken and turkey. Always!) There are established procedures for health and safety that are strictly enforced in markets and butchers across the United States but one can never be too careful. Almost all stomach related illness is caused by some sort of food borne bacteria. When you have control of the situation it seems wise to avoid making yourself sick.

# Index

# R

## W

Walnuts  32, 188
White Wine  52, 79, 82, 85, 100, 102, 112, 168, 170
Wine  21
Worcestershire Sauce  147

## Y

Yeast  119, 173
Yellow Peppers  166

## Z

Zest  82, 100, 108, 109, 111

Made in the USA
Lexington, KY
19 April 2012